NORMANS IN EUROPE

BY THE

REV. A. H. JOHNSON, M.A.

LATE FOLLOW OF ALL SOULS COLLEGE, OXFORD
HISTORICAL LECTURER TO TRINITY, ST. JOHN'S, PEMBROKE,
AND WADHAM COLLEGES

PREFACE.

The history of the Scandinavian Exodus which began in the ninth century falls conveniently into two periods.

During the first, (800 circ.—912) the people of Denmark, Sweden, and Norway harassed Europe with their inroads, and formed definite settlements in the British Isles, Russia, and France.

During the second, (1029-1066) France itself became the starting-place for a new series of incursions, led by men of Scandinavian descent, who had by that time adopted French customs and language. To this period belong the settlements in Spain and Italy, and the Norman conquest of England.

The aim of this book is to present a connected view of these incursions, and to bring clearly before the reader the important fact, that the Norman Conquest was only the last of this long series of settlements and conquests.

The narrow limits required by the character of the series have necessitated much compression.

Taking, therefore, the Norman Conquest as the centre of the book, I have contented myself with the briefest sketch of those settlements which do not intimately affect that event; and concentrating attention on that of the Seine, have sketched its fortunes in some detail, and traced the growing connection between Normandy and England which resulted in the conquest of the latter country.

Finally, following the Normans to England, I have dwelt especially on their influence on our country and the principles of our government, and drawn out the relations of Norman England with France and Sicily.

Want of space alone has prevented me from dealing more particularly with the Norman settlement in Italy, one of the most interesting of all, and one which requires the more attention, because it has not been adequately treated of by any English writer. But the history of that island belongs to Italian and Eastern rather than to English history, and it is one important period of English history which I have attempted to illustrate.

In one respect I feel conscious of having departed somewhat from the rule of the series. There are more names than I could have wished. This I have found unavoidable: but to obviate as far as possible the difficulty which may thereby be caused to the young reader, I have added a few genealogies of the most important families.

I have also given a short list of the authorities which may be useful to those who would extend their studies.

In conclusion, I would offer my best thanks to Professor Stubbs for much kind advice and invaluable criticism.

OXFORD: *March*, 1877.

THE NORMANS IN EUROPE.

CHAPTER I.
THE NORTHMEN IN THEIR HOME.

If we would thoroughly appreciate the importance of the Northmen and their influence on Europe, we must realise the wide extent of their conquests and settlements. To treat of the conquest of England by the Normans as an isolated event would be entirely to obscure its real meaning and effect; and this is equally true of the other settlements of the Northmen.

Leaving their Northern homes in the ninth century, they had by the end of the twelfth penetrated into nearly every country of Europe. So close were their political and family relations with all the countries of the West, from Iceland to Constantinople, from Russia to Spain, during the tenth, eleventh, and twelfth centuries, that a history of the Northmen is little short of a history of Europe during those ages. The great Exodus of the Scandinavian peoples which began in the ninth century, must accordingly be treated as a whole—and such will be the object of this book.

Again, it must be remembered that the three Northern countries of Denmark, Norway, and Sweden all shared in the general movement, and that the expeditions were often joined indiscriminately by Dane and Swede and Norseman.

It will be well, therefore, to direct our attention in the first instance to these three countries, and obtain as accurate a knowledge of the condition of Northmen in their home as is possible from the scanty evidence which exists.

Denmark, Sweden, and Norway were, in the eighth century, inhabited by a people called the 'Northmen,' a name universally used to describe the inhabitants of the Scandinavian continents.

These Northmen were, there is little doubt, closely akin to the Jutes, Angles, and Saxons, who had left their homes on the shores of the German Ocean some five centuries before for England,—branches therefore of the great Teutonic family of the Indo-European or Aryan race, which, coming originally from the East, broke in upon the Roman Empire, and overwhelmed the earlier Keltic or Finnish tribes who preceded them.

That this people should have turned north rather than south, that they should have occupied the inhospitable regions of the Scandinavian continents in preference to the more accessible lands to the south of them, may, at first, appear extraordinary. But, apart from the probability that they were forced northwards by the pressure ensuing on the general migration of the Gothic races and their conflict with the Roman Empire, the fact is not hard to explain on other grounds. These continents, Norway, Sweden, and Denmark, with all their apparent savageness, offered to a people of hunters better opportunities for supporting life, than the trackless forests of

Germany. The land abounded in animals which could be more easily captured in the broken country of the North than in the dense forests and wide plains of Germany. The rivers and fiords teemed with fish and wild-fowl; fossil belemnite and other stones used for weapons in an early state of society, are said to abound on the Norwegian coast; and Sweden was singularly rich in iron and copper ore, which lay very near the surface. Everything, in fact, required by people in an early state of civilisation was to be found there.

Of the condition of the Northmen at the time of their first settlement we can assert nothing. We do not know whether they had already passed out of the hunting stage and become a pastoral people, nor can we mark the date at which this condition was abandoned for the more fixed one which marks the rise of the agricultural system. The analogy of all other tribes of which we have any historical evidence would lead us to suppose that they had, at some time, passed through these stages. But, when we first meet with them, they had certainly become an agricultural people, and dwelt in settled homes.

The origin of society amongst the Northmen, in common with the rest of the Germanic peoples, is probably to be sought in the 'village community,' an association founded on the real or fictitious tie of the family. According to this system, the district occupied by each community was the common possession of the family or tribe, in whom the absolute ownership resided, and was divided into three parts: the village, the arable 'land,' and the common pasture. In the village, each of the tribal members had his homestead. Of the arable lands he had a right to a share, but he had to follow the prescribed rotation in his crops, and, when it was to lie fallow, changed his plot for another. On the pasture lands he might turn out his cattle, and cut his fire-wood, and when they were taken up for hay, each marks-man would have his hay-field. Thus the tribes-man was the tenant rather than the owner, and individual proprietorship, as we have it, was unknown. Each village community would have its assembly, in which every free mark-man enjoyed a right to sit, and here the petty laws which regulated the self-governing body would be passed.

This state of things, however, soon passed away. The improvement of agriculture led to the desire of a more permanent system of allotment, and with the rise of separate ownership, inequality of estate grew up. Thus, by the eighth century, the mark system had, partially, at least, disappeared.

Here, again, we are surrounded with difficulties arising from want of evidence. The Sagas are our only authority. Of these there exist two compilations, both of comparatively late date. 1. The elder Edda, a collection of the Sagas (lays), handed down from heathen times, and compiled about 1090 by a Christian priest of Iceland, Saemund Sigfusson by name. 2. The younger Edda, a prose mythology, written in the thirteenth century by, or under the direction of, Snorro Sturleson, another Icelander of noble family. In this, the old traditions gathered from the elder Edda and other Sagas, now lost, are strung together and given with matchless simplicity and pathos.

Though, then, we cannot be sure as to the exact date of the Sagas themselves, they most probably belong to the period anterior to the movement of the Scandinavian people, and contain the traditions of the earlier condition of their ancestors. The following description of Scandinavian society is that which has impressed itself upon the scalds or rhymers. They speak of society as divided into two classes. 1. The unfree—This class, arising after the mark system had died out and the land had been to some extent divided, enjoyed personal freedom, but no civil rights. They did not hold land, nor were they entitled to sit in the local assemblies. They formed a body of labourers, and were in many cases the personal followers of those above them. 2. The odal proprietors, or yeomen, formed a numerous body of small landowners, and were the only aristocracy. These were the original members of the old village community, who had established their right of individual ownership. They held their land in absolute proprietorship, and owed no taxes or dues to the Government beyond the bare necessity of contributing to the defence of their country. Any land yet undivided remained the common property of the tribe, and was 'leased' out to these odal proprietors on varying terms of tenure.

The political organization was based upon the mark system, which here left more enduring traces. Each village formed a separate community with its village assembly, in which the odal proprietor, or yeoman, enjoyed an inalienable right of sitting. Summoned to these 'Things,' as they were called, by a "Bod," or stick, which was passed from house to house, they there in concert managed the affairs of the district.

Each village had its village thing, and headman, and enjoyed considerable independence. A number of village communities formed a small tribal State, with its own petty king and assembly, larger than the village 'thing.'

The assemblies of the states and villages enjoyed together a supreme legislative, judicial, and administrative authority, the greater 'things' assuming the legislative and judicial, the lesser, the administrative functions within their respective spheres. So that the village thing 'would be bound to carry out the laws made, or the sentences passed, by the assembly, or 'thing,' of the state, just as an English Town Council is bound to carry out the provisions of an Act of Parliament at the present day, while the village 'thing' would have smaller matters under its own control just as the Town Council has. Lastly, these states were sometimes, though not necessarily, loosely united in a semi-federal union.

The kings of the tribal states were generally taken from a noble family, sometimes representing the kingly line in virtue of a supposed descent from Odin. Their office was in many cases partly hereditary, though probably, as with the Anglo-Saxons, elective within the limits of the privileged family. Their power was balanced by the assemblies of the state and village, without the concurrence of which they could perform no important act. Still, the king was not a mere nonentity. He presided in the assemblies and over the administration of justice; he officiated in the sacrificial feasts, led the host to war, and, as in all early societies, the personal influence of a powerful king would extend his authority far beyond its theoretical limits.

Feudal aristocracy there was none. The proud Northern yeoman would brook no superior, and the physical and historical circumstances of their country prevented the growth of any such caste. The comparative barrenness of the soil—small pasture lands cooped in on all sides by rugged rocks, and separated by deep fiords—could not afford sufficient produce to furnish a rent to a great lord over and above the sustenance required by the occupier of the soil, while the isolation of these fertile spots fostered the independence of each family. The hard primary rocks of the Scandinavian continents were unfit for building purposes, and no baron's castle rose to overawe the neighbourhood. Kings and people alike dwelt in wooden houses, which could easily be stormed and burnt.

The physical peculiarities of the country were aided by other circumstances. The absence of the law of primogeniture hindered the accumulation of large properties in one hand. At a later date the surplus population was drawn off by successive colonisations, while the levelling influence of war was not wanting to call forth individual merit, and to beat down the exclusive privileges of any one class. In the absence of writing, no learned class monopolised the management of state and village affairs, or pursued their studies in a literary language unknown to the lower classes, as was the case among the Anglo-Saxons in

England, where the churchmen often wrote in Latin.

As in all early societies, the prosecution of offenders was left to the individual or to his kith and kin. Pecuniary compensations were resorted to in all cases, the state merely assessing the sum; but in the case of greater offences, the blood-fine might be refused when it was deemed dishonourable to the kith of the injured man if his death or wrong were not revenged. This rough and ready system of justice explains many of the bloody struggles of those times.

For the mythology of the Scandinavians, we must again turn to the elder and the younger Eddas. And this is what we there learn. In the beginning of time, when yet there was naught, two regions lay on each side of chaos. To the north Niflheim, the abode of mist and snow and cloud and cold. To the south, Muspell, where it is so hot and bright that it burns, and none may tread save those who have an heritage there. The king of that land is Surtr, who guards the land with a flaming sword. When the hot blasts from Muspell met the cold rime and frost that came out of Niflheim, the frost melted by the might of Surtr, and became a great giant, Ymir, the sire of all the frost giants. But, besides the giant, the ice-drops as they melted formed a cow, on whose milk Ymir fed; and as she licked the stones covered with rime, a man named Buri arose, who was the father of Odin and his brethren. These are the Æsir, or good gods, and between these and the frost giants war arose, till at last Ymir was slain and all his race but one. From this one the later race of frost giants sprang.

With the body of the giant Odin made the world. The sea and waters are his blood; earth his flesh; the rocks his bones; pebbles his teeth and jaws. His skull was raised aloft and the heavens were made of it. The clouds are his brains. But the sun and moon and stars are formed of the fires which came out of Muspell. These Odin fixed in the heavens, and ordered their goings. Odin, the father of all (*Allfadir*), next made man, and gave him a soul which shall never perish, though the body shall decay.

Odin was the greatest of the gods. Next to him comes Frigga, his wife, who knows the fate of all men, though she never reveals it. Then Thor, his first-born son—the Thunderer, the chiefest of gods for strength, the sworn foe of the old frost giants, the tamer and queller of all unholy things.

Next Baldr, of fairest face and hair, the mildest-spoken of the gods, the type of purity and innocence.

These, with Freyr, who rules over rain and sunshine and the fruitfulness of the earth; and Freyia, the goddess of love; and many others, live in Midgard, the centre of the earth. Here they have built themselves a castle, Asgard, high above the earth; whence they can see all that goes on among mortals. Here the good shall live with Odin after death—while the wicked shall go to Niflheim (hell), the place of darkness and of cold.

But these simple myths were mingled with those of a more savage and sterner character,

Odin is not The All-father alone, but the God of battle (*Valfadir*) as well; and as such is worshipped by bloody sacrifices. Instead of the peaceful after-life in Midgard, men look forward to Valhalla, where those who die in battle shall feast with Odin. There their pastime shall be to fight with each other from dawn till meal-time, when they ride back to Valhalla and sit down to drink. Those who die of sickness or old age shall go to hell; the murderers, and those who forswear themselves, to Ná—a region formed of adders' backs wattled together, whose heads spit venom and form streams in which these shall wade for ever.

Meanwhile among the gods there is strife and woe. Of the children of the old frost giants, one Loki had been fostered by Odin, and brought up among his children, to their ruin. Fair of face is he, but a traitor, ill-tempered, deceitful, and of fickle mood.

With the rise of the traitor the golden age of the Æsir, or good gods, is at an end, and the old quarrels between them and the frost giants begin again. Yet so long as Baldr lived, sin and wickedness could not prevail on earth, nor could the ancient giant race triumph over the Æsir. To kill Baldr, therefore, was Loki's constant aim, and by treachery he succeeded. The gods, warned by the soothsayers that Baldr was doomed to die, made him free from death by sickness, or stones or trees, or beast or bird; and, rejoicing in their triumph, found harmless pastime in shooting at Baldr and smiting him with stones, while he remained unharmed. One tree, the mistletoe, they had not named, and Loki, making arrows of it, gave them into the hands of Hodr, the blind god. Armed with these weapons, he joined with his brethren in the sport, and shooting, slew fair Baldr, who went to hell. Loki, indeed, fell before the vengeance of Thor, but the doom of the gods was sealed; and heralded by three winters with no summer in between, 'the twilight of the gods 'drew on.

Then *Surtr*, the primeval god, should at last come forth, and hurling fire over the world, destroy the gods both good and bad. Then should arise another heaven, where the worthy dead should dwell with Surtr, and Baldr should thither return from hell.

Priests there were none: the king of the tribe or village took their place, and on the great festivals of the year, led the assembled men of the district in their religious ceremonies, and in the public business of the state with which the festal days were closed.

Such, as far as we can judge from the scanty evidence that we have, was the condition of the Northmen in the eighth century.

At the end of the eighth century, the homely, simple character of their life was disturbed. The Sagas clearly speak of a severe convulsion of society; and though we cannot trust these later authorities in their details, they were probably correct as to facts. The ill-defined relations of the several petty states, to one another and to the village districts of which they were composed, prevented a stable system, and offered to ambitious chiefs tempting opportunities for aggression; whilst the barrenness of the soil was unable to supply the growing wants of a rapidly increasing population. Hence the rise of petty struggles which rapidly became universal, and distracted the land with civil discord. The more fortunate chieftains established their authority; the less fortunate, scorning to accept the position of dependents, took to the sea, their natural refuge, and, collecting the turbulent spirits round them, sought in a life of piracy the sustenance denied them in their home. It was now that Europe first began to hear the name of the dread Vikings (*Vic*, a bay or fiord), and to suffer from their piratical inroads. In England the Danes appear, and threaten her rising unity. Abroad, the Northmen hasten to avenge the conquests of the Saxons by the Emperor of the West, and Charles the Great wept to see the long boats of these the deadly foes of his empire and his race, as they swept the Mediterranean.

Meanwhile at home the successful chieftains, relieved in part of their more independent adversaries, were enabled, though by severe struggles, gradually to consolidate their power. Many modifications were introduced into the social and political condition of the people. Slavery increased, social equality was broken through, royalty throve at the expense of individual liberty: piracy was now considered an honourable pursuit: the character of the people was affected. Surrounded by daily warfare, they caught the spirit of the times and became more warlike.

These petty struggles, with their attendant results, occupy the history of the northern kingdoms until, towards the latter half of the ninth century, they are replaced by more systematic attempts at organisation.

Within a few years of each other, three men arose in the several kingdoms of Denmark, Norway, and Sweden—Gorm the Old, Harald Harfagr, and Eric—who attempt to overthrow the independent chieftains, and to establish their own undisputed authority. Of these, the history of Harald Harfagr, of Norway, may be taken as a type. The son of a petty prince in the south of Norway, he had sought a bride from the court of a neighbouring chieftain. The maiden returned the contemptuous answer that she would not throw herself away on a king who had but a few districts for a kingdom, and added the taunt that it was strange no prince in Norway could make the whole country subject to him as Gorm the Old had done in Denmark, and Eric at Upsal. Incited by this spirited reply, Harald swore a solemn vow never to clip or comb his hair until he had subdued the whole of Norway, or to die in the attempt; 'and forthwith,' says the Saga, 'he devoted his life to this great aim.' His object was not gained without a struggle. The petty chieftains, united by their common danger, fought desperately and long; but Harald, aided by his own personal ability, and fortunately served by some of the best swords of the day, defeated them in a succession of severe encounters, and thus fulfilling his vow, gained his kingdom and his bride.

Of the petty chieftains, many had fallen in battle, scorning to live on in disgrace; a few became his dependents, and ruled their once independent possessions as his vice-regents. Most left their native shores, and sought in other lands the power they had lost at home. The movement thus begun was furthered by the means resorted to by Harald in organising his newly-won domain. In the preceding times, the Vikings had not confined their piratical incursions to foreign lands; they had plundered their own country as well, and preyed on kith and kin. Now, Harald adopted vigorous measures to put down this piracy; the turbulent spirits, driven from their own shores, swelled the forces of the exiled chieftains. His measures affected also the peaceable proprietors who had hitherto stayed at home. The expenses of government necessarily increasing with its centralisation, he was forced to raise money. This he did, not only by appropriating the common lands hitherto the undivided property of the collective tribe, and by transferring all taxes and fines paid into the common treasury of the tribe or to the chieftain, to the royal coffers, but also by imposing taxes on those who, till then, had held their land in full and free ownership. Irritated at this loss of their freedom, and in some cases perhaps unable to wring sufficient produce from the sterile soil, many of these, the backbone of the Northern people, joined the other discontented spirits, and furnished an element of stability and organisation hitherto unknown in the expeditions of the Vikings.

Then a movement, as yet unheard of, began. Denmark and Sweden, subjected under Gorm and Eric, probably experienced a similar convulsion, and a general exodus of the Northern people commenced.

It is material to note the difference between this later movement and the earlier ones which had preceded it. These were little more than marauding expeditions for the sake of plunder.

The pirates sailed the seas, pounced down upon any defenceless point, harried, sacked, and burnt the place, and were off again before any resistance could be organised. They had no idea of forming any definite settlement, and ravaged the territories of mend and foe alike. But now all this changes. The idea of definite settlement becomes apparent. The expeditions are joined, as we have seen, by a different class—proprietors robbed of their land and rights (as they, no doubt, deemed them), men to whom plunder for plundering's sake was distasteful, and who were anxious to find a peaceable home elsewhere—these are the class of men who now take the lead, and organise the hitherto aimless ravages of their countrymen. Hence it is that the invasions of the Northmen, always ushered in by plundering incursions, about this time change their character, and take the form of permanent settlements. Thus in England, the Danish invasions, which had been going on since 787, assumed a new form in 855, and the country was finally divided between Alfred and the Danes in 878. In France the interest is seen to centre round fewer leaders, who are evidently aiming at settlement, and already the Seine has become the favourite scene of action; while the Orkneys, Shetlands, Faroe Islands, Iceland, Russia now probably receive their new colonists.

CHAPTER II.
THE INVASIONS OF THE NORTHMEN.

We have now arrived at the point when we must leave the shores of the northern continent and follow the exiles in their several conquests and settlements. These naturally fall into two periods:—

1. 787-855. During which the invasions are little more than plundering raids.

2. 855-912. A period of conquest and definite settlement.

On the earlier period we need not long dwell. The incursions were of necessity only temporary in their effects, and were chiefly confined to England, Germany, and France, though Spain and even Italy were by no means free from attack.

Of these the Danish invasions of England, the best authenticated, scarcely come within the scope of our subject. Their attacks on Italy and Spain, though no doubt severe, led to no permanent results till a much later date, while in Germany and France their annals are rendered irremediably defective through the insufficiency of contemporary authorities. From the death of the chronicler Nithard, grandson of Charles the Great, a Count of Ponthieu, who fell fighting against the Northmen, and left a fragment abruptly ended by his death, the authorities are very scant and the information confused. The frequent repetition of particular names running over a period longer than that generally covered by the deeds of one man, renders it probable that the terror of a name lasted after the hero's death, and led the ecclesiastical chroniclers, never very well informed of events unconnected with their own district, to attribute to one the deeds of many.

All that we can feel certain of, all at least which it is in any way important to remember, is the frequency and enormous area of the attacks, and this cannot be put in better words than those of Sir Francis Palgrave:—'Take,' he says, 'the map, and cover with vermilion the provinces, districts, and shores which the Northmen visited, as a record of each invasion, the colouring will have to be repeated more than ninety times successively before you arrive at the conclusion of the dynasty of Charles the Great. Furthermore, mark by the usual symbol of war, two crossed swords, the localities where battles were fought by the pirates, where they were defeated or triumphant, or where they pillaged, burned, or destroyed, and the valleys and the banks of the Elbe, Rhine and Moselle, Scheldt, Meuse, Somme and Seine, Loire, Garonne and Adour, and all the coasts and coast-lands between estuary and estuary, all the countries between river and streams will appear bristling as with chevaux de frise.' This will give us some idea of the invasions as far as Gaul and Germany are concerned; but it should be repeated for England, Scotland, and the islands which surround their coasts to give any adequate conception of the misery they caused.

Confining, then, our attention more particularly to the second period, let us briefly consider the appearance and characteristic qualities of these Northmen.

The outward look of the Norse, the Dane, the Norseman was much the same. Broad-shouldered, deep-chested, long-limbed, yet with slender waist and small hands and feet, their figures told of strength; and so necessary was strength considered that puny infants were exposed and left to die, the healthy children being alone preserved. Their complexion—their hair and eyes, were fair—and the fair alone could pass for beautiful or well-born. A dark complexion was considered the mark of an alien race, and dishonourable. Thus Baldr, the noblest of the gods, was fair, and the outward appearance of the slave was thus contrasted with that of the freeman. Black and ugly they are. Their forefather, Thrall, had a broad face, bent back, long heels, blistered hands, stiff, slow joints, and clumsy figure. His wife, Thy, is bandy-legged, flat-nosed, and her arms are brown with toiling in the sun. Their children are like them.

The ordinary dress of both sexes was nearly the same. A shirt, loose drawers, long hose, high shoes with thongs twisted up the ankle. A short kirtle girt at the waist served for coat or gown; an armless cloak, with a low-crowned, broad brimmed hat, completed the dress of the man. The woman, instead of the hat, wore a wimple of linen, and over that a high twisted cap, sometimes bent at the top into the shape of a horn, but otherwise dressed much as the men. The under-clothing of both sexes was of linen; their outer of coarse, woollen homespun—of grey, or black, or blue, or red, the most prized of all.

To this the chiefs added in the time of war a helm and shirt of mail, and all were armed with a long shield, protecting the whole body—white in time of peace, red in time of war—covered with leather, with iron rim and boss; spears of ashen shaft and iron point; axes; and, above all, the sword, the darling of the Northmen.

Their ships were long half-decked galleys, propelled by oars and sail. The waist, where the rowers sat, was low, that the oars might have free play. The bow and stern were high, and ended, the former in a beak or jaw, the latter in the tail of some beast. Dragons were the most commonly represented, and thus the ship looked like a huge monster on the sea, whose gaping jaws were held to bewitch the foe. The sails were gay with stripes of blue or green or red.

In the prow stood the warriors, and the vessel was driven stem on against the enemy: in the stern the chief, and behind him the helmsman, his helm inscribed with magic runes to charm away all evil. In action the rowers were protected by planks set up along the bulwarks, and all round the vessel ran a gangway, from whence they boarded the enemy's ship.

The character of these hardy Northmen was well suited to their future destiny.

The daily struggle for existence in an inhospitable climate had taught them fearlessness and ready wit in danger. From the absence of all aristocracy or other privileged class they had acquired a spirit of independence, a haughty and unbending character which prepared them for their future conquests. Set face to face with the mysteries of nature and of their self-taught religion, they had gained an heroic fancifulness, a thoughtful sternness which lit up the darker tints. These features were the natural result of the free and independent life of their forefathers. To these we must add a cold-blooded ferocity, contracted in the long civil disturbances which had torn their country since the end of the eighth century. All these are the qualities common in early times to successful conquerors; but, as we follow the history of their settlements, another more important feature appears, namely, their extraordinary versatility and power of adapting themselves to varied forms and states of society. The Northmen never seem to have been original, never to have invented anything; rather they readily assumed the language, religion, ideas of their adopted country, and soon became absorbed in the society around them. This will be found to be invariably the case, except with regard to Iceland, where the previous occupation was too insignificant to affect the new settlers. In Russia, they became Russians; in France, Frenchmen; in Italy, Italians; in England twice over Englishmen, first in the case of the Danes, and secondly, in that of the later Normans. Everywhere they became fused in the surrounding nationality. Their individuality is lost, and their presence is traced only in the nomenclature of the country, that fossil remnant of denationalised races, as it has been called. Not so their influence. They fell on stirring times, and in every case they took the lead, and deeply affected the nations with which they came in contact. Europe at that date was in a fluid state, and the Northmen seem to have acted as a crystallising power; to have formed a nucleus round which political society might grow. In Iceland they formed a free republic, in Russia they first organised a kingdom; in England they, by their pressure, first consolidated the kingdom of Wessex, then conquered it under Canute and William I.; in the West-Frankish country they finally put an end to the long struggle for supremacy, sounded the death knell of the Karolings of Laon, and aided to form modern France. Nor is this all; they borrow everything and make it their own, and their presence is chiefly felt in increased activity and more rapid development of institutions, literature, and art. Thus, while they invent nothing, they perfect, they organise everything, and everywhere appear the master-spirits of their age.

We have hitherto treated the Norwegians, Swedes and Danes under the common appellation of Northmen; and this is in many ways the most convenient, for it is often impossible to decide the nationality of the individual settlement. Indeed, it would appear probable that the devastating bands were often composed indiscriminately of the several nationalities. Still, in tracing the history of their conquests, we may lay it down as a general rule that England was the exclusive prey of the Danes; that Scotland and the islands to the north as far as Iceland, and to the south as far as Anglesea and Ireland fell to the Norwegians, and Russia to the Swedes; while Gaul and Germany were equally the spoil of the Norwegians and the Danes. The last will claim our more careful attention. At the former we can only cast a cursory glance.

I. In England, the Danish inroads beginning about the year 787, had assumed their second phase about the year 855, and destroyed the nascent unity of the kingdom then partially attained by Egbert, king of the West-Saxons. The Danes had easily occupied the more northern kingdoms of Northumbria, Mercia, and East Anglia; peopled as they were by the Angles, a race more nearly akin to their own than the Saxons, and disorganised by the late struggles for supremacy. But as they drew near to the more thoroughly organised kingdom of Wessex, the opposition became more resolute, and the struggle more severe. Led by their great hero, Alfred, the Saxons maintained the struggle for seven years, until the peace of Wedmore, 878, obtained for Wessex a respite from her harassing foe. By that peace England was divided into two nearly equal parts; Alfred holding all south of the Thames, Lea, and Watling Street; that is Kent, Sussex, Wessex, and part of Mercia; while he ceded all north of this to the Danes, and Guthrum, their leader, acknowledging his over-lordship, embraced Christianity as a condition of the peace.

Thus England was again divided, and her premature attempt at unity to all appearance indefinitely postponed.

Yet in truth the loss was apparent rather than real. By this peace the limits between the two people were fixed, and the Danes no longer continued their aggressions. Confined behind their self-constituted boundary, they soon began to amalgamate with the conquered people. Their leader having embraced Christianity, they gradually followed his example, and the northern Church, overthrown in the earlier days of the Danish invasions, was speedily revived.

Meanwhile, although temporarily a loss to England, the result of the Scandinavian invasions had been to consolidate Wessex. During the struggle she had been looked upon as the national leader of the English, and common perils and victories had fused the various Saxon tribes more completely than they had ever been before. The part of Mercia which remained to Wessex became completely incorporated with her, while the organisation of the country was systematised and perfected by the wise measures of Alfred and his successors. When the reaction came, Wessex stepped boldly forth and encroached upon the Danish districts. During the reigns of Alfred's powerful sons and grandsons the advance was rapid. The Danes themselves crushed out the local independence, and the Saxons inherited the results of their labours. When a hundred years are past, England, under Edgar the Peaceful, came forth more really united than ever before. The Danes had done their work, perhaps revived the institutions common to the North German race, breathed new life into the social and political condition of the country, and then, assimilating themselves rapidly to the conquered people, dropped into the common mass of Englishmen. A few traces of their presence alone remained in the modification of some official titles, in a few privileges and laws, and other local peculiarities which lasted in Danelagu (the land of Dane law) till the Norman conquest, and in the nomenclature of certain localities and towns.

II. While England had been overcome by the Danes, the Norwegians had turned their attention chiefly to the north of the British Isles and the islands of the West. Their settlements naturally fell into three divisions, which tally with their geographical position. 1. The Orkneys and Shetlands, lying to the N.E. of Scotland. 2. The isles to the west as far south as Ireland. 3. Iceland and the Faroe Isles.

The Orkneys and Shetlands. Here the Northmen first appear as early as the end of the eighth century, and a few peaceful settlements were made by those who were anxious to escape from the noisy scenes which distracted their northern country. In the reign of Harald Harfagr they assume new importance, and their character is changed. Many of those driven out by Harald sought a refuge here, and betaking themselves to piracy periodically infested the Norwegian coast in revenge for their defeat and expulsion. These ravages seriously disturbing the peace of his newly acquired kingdom, Harald fitted out an expedition and devoted a whole summer to conquering the Vikings and extirpating the brood of pirates. The country being gained, he offered it to his chief adviser, Rögnwald, Jarl of Möri in Norway, father of Rollo of Normandy, who, though refusing to go himself, held it during his life as a family possession, and sent Sigurd, his brother, there, Sigurd, having organised his kingdom, crossed to the mainland, and overran Caithness and Sutherland, then, in common with the Orkneys and the Shetlands, inhabited by the North Picts, a tribe of Gaelic extraction. Sigurd's death was characteristic of his life. While carrying the head of a victim, Malbrede 'the bucktooth' swung at his saddlebow, he was wounded in the leg by the prominent teeth of his lifeless foe, and died from the effects. Although his ally, Thorstein Olaveson, gained Caithness and Sutherland, on the direct failure of his issue, authority was again in abeyance and the Vikings again commenced their ravages. Rögnwald next sent his son Einar, and from, his time we may date the final establishment of the Jarls of Orkney, who henceforth owe a nominal allegiance to the King of Norway. In the eleventh century the leading Jarl accepted Christianity at the peremptory demand of his sovereign, and soon after they finally conquered Caithness and Sutherland, and wrested a recognition of their claim from Malcolm II. of Scotland. Their influence was continually felt in the dynastic and other quarrels of Scotland; the defeat of Duncan, in 1040, by the Jarl of Orkney, contributing not a little to Duncan's subsequent overthrow by Macbeth. They fostered the independence of the north of Scotland against the southern king, and held their kingdom until, in 1355, it passed by the female line to the house of Sinclair. The Sinclairs now transferred their allegiance to their natural master, the King of Scotland; and finally the kingdom of the Orkneys was handed over to James III. as the dowry of his bride, Margaret of Norway.

III. The close of the eighth century also saw the commencement of the incursions of the Northmen in the west of Scotland, and the Western Isles soon became a favourite resort of the Vikings. In the Keltic annals these unwelcome visitors had gained the name of Fingall, 'the white strangers,' from the fairness of their complexion; and Dugall, the black strangers, probably from the iron coats of mail worn by their chiefs. From the intermixture of the Kelts and Northmen sprang a race called the Gall-Gael, who joined the Northmen in their raids, or plundered on their own account. In the year 795 we find them sacking the monastery of Iona, once the centre of religious vitality in the North.

By the end of the ninth century a sort of naval empire had arisen, consisting of the Hebrides, parts of the western coasts of Scotland, especially the modern Argyllshire, Man, Anglesea, and the eastern shores of Ireland.

This empire was under a line of sovereigns who called themselves the Hy-Ivar (grandsons of Ivar), and lived now in Man, now in Dublin. Thence they often joined their kinsmen in their attacks on England, and at times aspired to the position of Jarls of the Danish Northumbria. It may seem strange that a kingdom so widely scattered should have held together; but the sea was their highway, and by it communication was far easier at that date than by land.

Moreover, it is probable that the independence of the several isles was greater than the scanty records which we have allow.

At the close of the tenth and beginning of the eleventh century the battles of Tara and Clontarf overthrew the power of these Norsemen (or Ostmen as they were called) in Ireland, and restored the authority of the native Irish sovereign. About this time they became Christians, and in the year 1066 we find one of their princes joining Harald Hardrada of Norway in his invasion of England, which ended so disastrously in the battle of Stamford Bridge. Magnus of Norway, thirty-two years later, after subduing the independent Jarls of Shetland and the Orkneys, attempted to reassert his supremacy along the western coast. But after conquering Anglesea, whence he drove out the Normans who had just made a settlement there, he crossed to Ireland to meet his death in battle. The sovereignty of the Isles was then restored to its original owners, but soon after split into two parts—the Suderies and Norderies (whence the term Sodor and Man), north and south of Ardnamurchan Point.

The next glimpse we have of these dominions is at the close of the twelfth century, when we find them under a chief named Somarled, who exercised authority in the islands and Argyleshire, and from him the clans of the Highlands and the Western Isles love to trace their ancestry. After his death, according to the Highland traditions, the islands and Argyleshire were divided amongst his three sons. Thus the old Norse empire was finally broken up, and in the thirteenth century, after another unsuccessful attempt by Haco, King of Norway, to re-establish the authority of the mother kingdom over their distant possessions, an attempt which ended in his defeat at the battle of Largs by the Scottish king, Alexander III., they were ceded to the Scottish kings by Magnus IV., his son, and an alliance was cemented between the two kingdoms by the marriage of Alexander's daughter, Margaret, to Eric of Norway.

IV. Meanwhile the Northmen had discovered Iceland. The first discoverers were a Viking named Naddod, and Gardar, a Swede; and they, returning home, praised the land. They had climbed a high fell on the eastern side to see if there were any signs of men—but saw none. The friths, they said, were full of fish. In some of the fields in the summertime butter dropped from every blade of grass. But the winter was cold, and towards the north they had seen frith after frith packed with drift ice. Hence they called it Iceland. It was evidently a secluded place, quiet, and scarce trodden by the foot of man. When therefore Harald Harfagr had driven the peaceful proprietors from their home, by his heavy hand, and had even subdued the Orkneys and the Shetlands, those who were weary of these feuds sailed north to Iceland and Faroe, and sought rest in those quiet lands. Ingolf Arnavson came first, in 874, and settled at Rykyavik; and others soon followed him. Thus the colonisation of Iceland seems to differ somewhat from the other settlements of the Northmen.

The few inhabitants found there, probably Kelts, did not offer much opportunity for spoil; and the least warlike of the Northmen were attracted thither. To Iceland they transferred their system of clan government, which they had enjoyed in Norway before the rise of the domestic feuds, and established it with some modifications.

The country was well suited to such a state of society, cut up as it is by desert tracts and raging watercourses; where each valley is separated from the next by lonely heaths, snow-clad fells, and plains of barren lava.

As the number of the colonists increased, however, changes were introduced. Over the district assemblies an All-thing was established. This, the common Assembly for the whole island, met in the plain of the All-thing, in the south of the country. A code was drawn up, and a Lawman elected as President of the Assembly. Here laws were passed, and private suits eventually decided before judges appointed by the Lawman. If the parties were not satisfied, a last appeal lay to their trial combat. These were fought on an island in the river hard by, and were regulated by a code of honour.

The executive was entrusted to a 'Court of Laws' (*Lögretta*), the members of which were the Lawman and Court of twelve judges of district courts or assemblies, who were chieftains and priests besides. This Court of Laws, sitting in the Hall of Laws—declared the law, voted public grants, elected the Lawman, and decided questions affecting the community at large.

Thus, practically, the government was an aristocratic republic; and the real power lay in the hands of the chief men of each district, who alone could be judges, the Lawman, and members of the Court of Laws.

Every freeman might indeed challenge their decisions, and by his simple prohibition render the decrees of the Court of Laws illegal; but by this he was sure to incur the wrath of the powerful families, and the right was not often exercised. The power was, there is no doubt, virtually in the hands of an aristocracy; and the abolition of combat on the introduction of Christianity in the eleventh century, placed the freemen still more in the hands of the judges and their assessors; but their condition was at least superior to that of their class in other countries at that date: individual freedom was but little interfered with, and their life seems to have been prosperous and happy. It was here that the Scandinavian literature was preserved, and, as before mentioned, that the elder and younger Eddas were compiled by Soemund Sigfusson and Snorro Sturleson.

From Iceland the Northmen discovered Greenland, and settled there in 981. Perhaps the reason for this may be found in the gradual increase of aristocratic privilege in Iceland, However that may be, a prosperous colony was established there, which lasted until the colonists were all destroyed by the great plague which swept over Europe in the fourteenth century; and, if the traditions be true, some sailed thence and discovered Vinland or America.

Meanwhile, in Iceland, the power of the chieftains increased, and—a sure sign of this—in the latter half of the twelfth century jealousies sprang up between them. Then the prosperity of the colony rapidly declined, and, in the middle of the thirteenth century it was occupied by the King of Norway, and the republic destroyed.

V. The settlement of the Northmen in Russia is too large a subject, and lies so far out of our way that the briefest notice must suffice.

While the Western Seas had been the scene of the exploits chiefly of the Danes and Norsemen, the Swedes had taken to the Baltic, and spoiled or levied tribute from the Sclavonic tribes along the coast.

In the year 862, Ruric, a Swede, was called in by the Sclavonic tribes to settle their disputes. 'Our land is large and rich,' the suppliants said, 'but order in it there is none. Do ye come and rule over us.' Ruric, thus invited, came, and occupied Novgorod, while his followers settled at Kief.

After Ruric's death, Oleg, his kinsman and guardian of his young son Igor, overcame the independent princes of Kief, which henceforth became the capital of Russia. Here, rapidly amalgamating with their subjects, the descendants of Ruric long held the title of Grand Prince.

In the tenth century they established commercial relations with Constantinople. Sailing down the Dnieper, they reached the Euxine and the Hellespont; and in the markets of Constantinople exchanged the commodities of the North—furs, hides, and slaves—for the corn, wine, and oil of the sunny South.

The riches of the empire soon excited their jealousy, and these friendly relations were exchanged for those of enmity. In a period of 190 years, the Russians made four attempts to plunder the Imperial city, and though eventually unsuccessful, were only defeated under the very walls. 'They dragged,' we are told, 'their ships ashore, and mounting them on wheels sailed on dry land up to the gates.'

At the end of the tenth century Vladimir, the descendant of Oleg and then Grand Prince of Russia, married the sister of the Eastern Emperor Basil, and became a convert to Christianity. The Sclavonic translations of the Scriptures, written by Cyril and Methodius in the ninth century, passed into Russia and became the national Bible of the Russians.

During the reign of his descendant Yaroslaf, the connexion between the princely house of Russia and the Scandinavians of the West was close. St. Olaf of Norway and the Russian prince had both married daughters of Olaf, King of Sweden. At his court the saint had found a refuge when driven out by Canute of England;

> 'King Olaf eastward over the sea
> To Russia's monarch had to flee:'

and on Olaf's final defeat and death at the battle of Sticklestad, his only son, Magnus, found a shelter at his uncle's court, whence he returned to overthrow Sweyn, the son of Canute, and regain the throne of Norway. Hither, too, another fugitive had come—Harald Hardrada, the half-brother of St. Olaf, who, though only a boy of fifteen, had fought in the battle of Sticklestad.

Since the beginning of the tenth century, the Emperors of the East, anxious to secure the assistance of these stalwart warriors of the North, had enticed some of them south and formed them into a body-guard under the name of the Varangians, (Vár, oath—Væringjar—βάραγγοι). Bound by an oath to the Emperor, and placed under a strict military code, they enjoyed great privileges. They kept watch at the door of the imperial bedchamber, and lodged in the palace itself; and at the death of the Emperor had the curious privilege of roaming at will through the imperial treasury and carrying off what they would.

To Constantinople Harald came, and, in the service of the Emperor, led the Varangian Guard against the Saracens in Egypt and Syria, thus anticipating the future deeds of the Normans in the Crusades; and saw Greece and Italy, where he fought with his distant kinsmen the Normans, who were already settled in Italy.

In this service he gained a wide-spread fame and amassed an enormous treasure. Then, quarrelling with his master the Emperor, he went back to Russia to marry Elizabeth, the daughter of Yaroslaf.

Thence he returned to Norway, to share that kingdom with Magnus the Good, his nephew, till the death of his rival left him the sole possession of the Norwegian throne.

Nineteen years afterwards, as we shall see, he crossed to England, to claim that kingdom from Harold, the son of Godwine, and to end his strange life at the battle of Stamford Bridge.

Meanwhile in Russia Yaroslaf had died, to be succeeded by Ysevold, and then by Bridge. Vladimir II., who once more came west for a bride, and married Githa, the daughter of the English Harold, Hardrada's foe.

Here we must take leave of Russia, still in the hands of the descendants of Ruric, who were to hold the crown for yet five hundred years.

CHAPTER III.
THE SETTLEMENT IN GAUL.

The great event of the ninth century is the fall of the ill-cemented empire raised by Charles the Great; that of the tenth, the rise of the national kingdoms of Germany, France, and Italy. In these two events the Northmen had their share; they rose with the fall of the Karolings, and became firmly established with the rise of modern France.

Their invasions, beginning about the year 799, ran very much the same course as those of the Danes in England, and about the same time changed their character from predatory incursions to definite settlements. Indeed, in many cases the invasions are contemporaneous, and the same names appear now in England, now abroad. We have already alluded to the wide extent of their devastations and the terror they inspired, but to understand in any way the miseries which Gaul, Germany, and Italy endured during this period, we must remember that these countries were torn by the most deadly internal feuds, which prevented any united action against the common foe. The children of Charles the Great were fighting for the spoils of his wide empire, and violating all right, justice, and plighted faith; other competitors were joining the strife and struggling for their share. The people, down-trodden, neglected, oppressed, or treated as so many conscripts who could be hurried to the battlefield, were grouping themselves for protection's sake round a host of greedy, selfish nobles, or sinking down and increasing the number of the slaves. Such was the internal condition of the countries—a meaningless, hopeless tale of hateful factions, which loads the memory and sickens the heart, and amid which only one important principle struggles to the surface—namely, the rising cry of nationality, protesting against these personal quarrels and selfish compacts, and demanding that the interest of people, and not of kings, should decide the boundaries of the land. Sadly was Europe expiating the attempt of Charles to raise an Empire of the West, an attempt which came too early or too late. Nor was this all. A triple scourge aggravated these self-inflicted sores. While the Northmen harassed the coasts and river shores, the Hungarian cavalry from the East swept over Germany, passed the Rhine, and penetrated as far as Vermandois and Provence; crossed the Alps, and devoured the Lombard plains. Meanwhile from the Mediterranean and from Spain the Saracens harassed the south of Gaul, and joined the Hungarians in Provence and the Alps. Of the condition of the lower classes we know but little. History has recorded the cruelties, the virtues, the honours and dishonours, the victories, the defeats of the great; but about the poorer classes she is generally silent, or at best has but a stammering tale to tell. We may quote, however, the words of the later author of the Romance of Rollo: 'What do we see around? Churches burning, people slaughtered, through the weakness of the king. The Northmen wreak their will in France. From Blois to Senlis not a grain of corn, and no one dares to labour in field or vineyard. If war cease not, famine is at our doors.' This poem was not written till the twelfth century, but the author borrows from earlier writers, and we may believe that his words were true enough. Well might the choirs of the South chant their petition: 'From the arrows of the Hungarians may the Lord deliver us!' and those of the North answer in despairing cadence: 'From the fury of the Northmen save us. Lord!'

The incursions of the Northmen in Gaul naturally fall into three groups, guided by the great rivers and intervening shores. 1. The North Expedition, which includes the territories around the Rhine, the Scheldt, and the Elbe, the farthest southern point being the Neckar and the Rhine. 2. The districts of the Loire and Garonne, reaching as far west as Spain, and inland as far as Bourges. 3. Those of the Seine, Somme, and Oise.

The invasions of Gaul by the Northmen differ from those of England by the Danes in one material point. Numerous as they were, they were isolated and scattered; those of the Danes in England continuous. Consequently the latter permanently occupied one half of England, and, though becoming Englishmen, still retained a certain local existence, and remained more or less distinct until the Norman Conquest.

But the settlers in Gaul, lying in small, isolated groups, and but little recruited by new comers, soon became entirely merged in the surrounding nationality, and lost their individuality. Hence it is that one settlement alone that of Rollo at Rouen, in any sense survived, all the rest being rapidly lost to history. Even here it is not as Northmen but as Frenchmen that the settlers are important. The followers of Rollo became French and assumed the language, and so rapidly did the change occur, in the court at least, that the grandson of Rollo had to be sent to the district of Bayeux, which longest retained its Scandinavian character, to learn the language of his forefathers.

Remembering, then, that the incursions of the Northmen, though they had a terrible reality while they lasted, were but in few cases permanent in their result, we may at once dismiss all but the last.

The mouth of the Seine offered a tempting opening to the pirates as they skirted the shores of Gaul, and the commercial city of Rouen had early attracted their plundering expeditions. Gaining boldness, they pressed inland, and continually threatened Paris, then a town on the frontier of the kingdom of the West Franks, whose capital lay at Laon. So frequent were these piratical invasions that in 861 Charles the Bald granted the city and a large district round it to Robert the Strong as a March or border territory against the Northmen. From that day forth the destinies of Paris began to rise, at first against the Normans, and then in league with them, until, by the accession of Hugh Capet, she finally became the capital, and her Count the first king, of modern France.

Fifteen years afterwards, according to the chronicles, Rollo, the future Duke of Normandy, entered the Seine, and from that day till 912 ravaged the unfortunate country. This Rollo, termed the Ganger or Walker, because he was too tall and stout for any horse to bear, is, so far as his earlier exploits are concerned, somewhat a legendary hero. The son of Rögnwald, Jarl of Mori in Norway, he came of a family of Vikings. His brother-in-law, Einar, was, as we have seen, Jarl of the Orkneys. Rollo is described as following the calling of a Viking in Gaul and England for nearly forty years before his final settlement at Rouen. He is said to have joined Guthrum in his wars against Alfred, but to have been persuaded by the Saxon king to leave England, and seek richer spoil in France. His exploits are spread over so many years, that it seems likely that there were two men of the same name whose deeds have been confounded.

To add to our difficulty, there is a gap in the contemporary chronicles from 900 to 911. We must therefore be contented to leave him as we find him, a hero of romance, and follow the accounts left us by the chroniclers and sagas. In the year 888, the fatal year which saw the final dismemberment of the empire of Charles the Great, began the famous siege of Paris by Rollo. The town was, however, successfully defended by its Count, Eudes, who in reward was for a time chosen king of France. When the chroniclers speak again, we find Rollo in possession of Rouen, and Gaul in a pitiable state. In spite of his defeat by the Count of Paris, Rollo's devastations continued, until at last Charles the Simple granted him by treaty the territories which were already his own, and thus, as Alfred the Great had done for England, gained a respite for the distracted country. By this treaty of Clair on Epte, Rollo secured the country from the Epte to the sea, and the overlordship of Brittany, with the hand of Gisela, the daughter of Charles the Simple, and, accepting Christianity as the price of the treaty, was led to the font by Robert, Count of Paris, who consented to be his godfather. To the demand of Charles that Rollo should do homage to him and kiss his toe, the independent Northman answered indignantly, 'Ne si, by Got' (Not so, by God). When at last he consented that it should be done by proxy, it is said that King Charles was thrown backwards by the rudeness of the Danish soldier, as he raised his foot to kiss it. The tale probably points to a real act of homage done by Rollo; but the Normans of later date appealed to it to show that they held their country of no higher sovereign-in-chief, but of God alone, and were proud of an insult offered with impunity to a descendant of the great Emperor of the West.

As to the internal condition of the province after the occupation, it is impossible to speak with certainty. The land, we are told, was 'roped' out among his followers. Most probably the Northmen became the only land-owners, while the conquered race was reduced to a state of serfdom. The country seems to have been divided into counties, and bestowed upon the chief advisers of Rollo, but in the absence of written documents of any kind during the reigns of the first two dukes, it is idle to speculate on the political condition of the dukedom. The legend, which under various forms so often appears in many countries, that the duke's bracelets hung to a tree and, unguarded except by the terror of his name, remained untouched for full three years, attests the vigilance of his government. Towns and churches rose again under his paternal sway, and the fame of Rollo the pirate was soon lost in that of Rollo the legislator and father of his people.

Leaving Rollo definitely settled at Rouen, let us look around us and consider the condition of that part of Western Europe in which Rollo and his successors were to play so important a part. Geography, which in early times is history, had cried out against the empire of Charles the Great, and national aspirations triumphed at last. After the death of Charles III., who had for a moment reunited the dominions of the Emperor Charles the Great, the ill-assorted elements were for ever separated, and four kingdoms arose—1, Germany; 2, Italy; 3, Burgundy; 4, Gaul. Of these Germany fell into a kind of loose federation of four nations—Franconia, Saxony, Swabia, Bavaria, with their separate laws and their own dukes, each of which in turn gave a king to Germany. On the death of Arnulf, an illegitimate descendant of Charles the Great who had been chosen king, Conrad of Franconia, acknowledged by all the nations except Lotharingia, obtained the crown, and the same year which saw Rollo established in Normandy saw Germany transferred to her national kings. He was succeeded by Henry I., of the house of Saxony. Both these were descended by the female side from Charles the Great; but the rise of the power of Saxony, the emperor's most deadly foe, rather points to the final exclusion of his race from Germany.

Italy and the Empire, generally but not always hanging together, were tossed like shuttlecocks to and fro, until Otho I. descended from Germany and claimed the Imperial and the Iron Crown; and the Papacy, passing into the hands of a succession of infamous popes, the paramours and bastard sons of two shameless women, bade fair to lose all moral influence in Europe.

At this time there were two kingdoms of Burgundy. 1. Transjurane, consisting of North Savoy and all Switzerland between the Reuss and the Jura, then under one king named Rudolf. 2. Cisjurane Burgundy, consisting of Provence, Dauphiné, the south of Savoy, and the country between the Saône and the Jura, afterwards called The County of Burgundy, or Franche Comté. This kingdom, founded by Boso of Provence in 879, was then in the hands of his son Louis, who, after gaining the country west of the Rhone and most of Languedoc, had aspired to the dangerous bauble of the Empire. He was half blinded by his rival, Berengar, and returned home to live in retirement till his death. His dominions soon alter passed, with the exception of Dauphiné, to his more successful neighbour, and, under Rudolf II., became the kingdom of Arles.

Gaul, on the death of Charles III., becomes for just 100 years the object of contention between the last of the Karolings and the rising house of Capet, between the Imperial German-speaking city of Laon and the ducal French-speaking city of Paris. At first Eudes, Count of Paris, raised to fame by his successful defence of Paris against the Northmen, was chosen king, and although his rivals brought over the young Charles the Simple, the descendant of Charles the Great, from England, where he had been sent for safety, and got him crowned, the Count held his ground successfully death in 899. Then Charles quietly succeeded, and the kingdom of the West Franks was once more restored to the city of Laon. His kingdom was bounded to the south and north by the Mediterranean and the English Channel, and stretched east and west from the Meuse and the Rhone to the Pyrenees. In addition to this he held the Channel Islands and the County of Barcelona. But of this territory he was by no means actual master. Brittany and Aquitaine scarcely acknowledged his authority, and generally stood aloof, while nearer at home his power was overshadowed by four great feudatories who often set him at nought. In the south the duchy of Burgundy was held by Richard the Justiciar. In the north the County of Flanders, formed as a March by Charles the Bald against the Northmen, was now under Baldwin the Bold, a powerful and turbulent vassal, quarrelling with everyone, and disturbing the peace even of the royal domain itself

At Paris, another March, Robert, Duke of France, the brother of the king's late rival Eudes, the deadly foe of his race and name, ruled over the greater part of Central Gaul north of the Loire, and, as was then not unfrequently the case, enjoyed considerable wealth as lay Abbot of St. Denis and St. Germain of Paris, and of St. Martin of Tours. Even the narrow extent of the royal domain, composed of a small district round the city of Laon and Compiègne, was threatened in the north by Herbert II. of Vermandois. This powerful Count, descended from Pepin the son of Charles the Great, and holding the rich territories of Rheims, Soissons, Senlis, St. Quentin and Peronne, claimed a purer and more certain descent from the Emperor than Charles himself, and was only biding his time to become the gaoler, and perhaps the murderer, of his king. Lastly came the Metropolitan bee of Rheims, lying within the territories of Vermandois, yet independent. Its primate was the Prince Bishop of France, and its possession was a continual bone of contention between the rival princes. Gaul, in fact, was a loose collection of powerful princes owing a purely nominal allegiance to their suzerain, which they discarded whenever their interests clashed. Perhaps it may be said that

Charles was more really master of German Lotharingia which, refusing to acknowledge the upstart Conrad of Franconia, paid a temporary but personal allegiance to him as the representative of the Karoling line. Already had Charles's authority been disputed by these turbulent feudatories, and the quarrel had apparently only been discontinued owing to the renewed invasions of the Northmen which preluded the settlement of Duke Rollo at Rouen.

Such was the condition of Gaul at the time of the treaty of Clair on Epte. By this treaty one more dangerous vassal was admitted within the realm, but the immediate result was a decided gain to Charles. Plainly it Avas at the expense of the Dukes of Brittany and of Paris that the cession was made. Charles resigned a territory over which he had but little power, and the two first Norman dukes fully repaid the gift by heartily supporting Charles throughout the rest of his troubled life.

The common danger from the Northmen once removed, the quarrels again broke out. Charles, by the spontaneous allegiance of Lotharingia and by the aid of the Northmen, had gained an increase of strength, and jealousy perhaps was the immediate cause of the rebellion. A strong coalition arose. Robert of Paris was chosen king, leaning on the united powers of Vermandois and Burgundy. Yet

Charles, aided by the people of Lotharingia, by Rollo and some Northmen who had settled on the Loire, was strong enough to win a great battle at Soissons, where Robert paid the penalty with his life. Hugh the Great, his son, might well have aspired to the crown. But now, as throughout his life, he preferred the less dangerous position of the king-maker, and Rudolf of Burgundy, his brother-in-law, accepted the dangerous post. Charles the Simple, trusting himself to the plighted troth of Herbert of Vermandois, and placing himself in his power, was faithlessly seized and kept a prisoner, with one short interval, until his death. In revenge, Rollo ravaged the country of the Duke of Paris, and a long war of four years ensued, generally to the advantage of the Norman duke.

This, though it did not open the prison to the royal captive, added two important acquisitions to the Norman territory. The Bessin, the district round Bayeux, was granted to Rollo, as well as the land of Maine. The claim to the latter was left for Rollo's successors to enforce, but of the former he gained immediate possession, and it henceforth formed the most important portion of the duchy. A Saxon colony had existed there since the later days of the Roman empire, and alone of the Teutonic settlements had resisted the absorbing influence of the Romance element. Now, reinforced by the new settlement of a kindred race, it maintained its Teutonic character and speech. In the reign of Rollo's successor it formed the nucleus of a rebellion of the non-Romanised element of the duchy against the other, then become thoroughly French. To it his grandson was sent to learn the pure language of his fathers, and to this day it retains many features of its Saxon and Scandinavian origin.

The annexation of the Bessin was the last exploit of Rollo. Shortly afterwards, at the demand of his people, he resigned, though unwillingly, in favour of his son. Five years more, it is said, he lived, and then the old man of fourscore and odd years—years teeming with deeds of strange contrast, of stranger import to future times—disappears from history. As we stand over his tomb in the chapel of St. Romanus at Rouen, strange are the thoughts which flit across our mind. Here lies the once dread Viking, the pillager of France; then one of the most powerful of her sons, a duke, a legislator; the father of his people, the progenitor of along line of dukes and kings. When all is told, we know but little of him. Many of the rolls which would have recorded his fame were probably burnt by his own hand. To recall all the events of his varied life is now beyond the power of man; but the best proof of his power and his genius is, that it was his life that inspired a canon of his own town Bayeux to write one of the earliest romances of modern Europe, and that while all other settlements of the race in France and Germany rapidly disappeared, his alone has lasted on and deeply affected future ages.

CHAPTER IV.
WILLIAM LONGSWORD.

The change of rulers at Rouen in no way altered the attitude of parties with regard to the question of the crown. Charles the Simple lived till 929, when he died in prison—as some said, poisoned. By this event Rudolf should have been left in quiet enjoyment of his throne, but this was not the object of Herbert of Vermandois, whose support of him had all along been selfish. Herbert's one aim had been to weaken the royal power and increase his own. While, therefore, Charles lived, he was the liegeman of Rudolf; when Charles died Rudolf was his bitterest enemy. Nor were the other great men of France much better. The difference was of degree, not of kind. If Herbert was perjured and faithless, Hugh was a designing, ambitious man, refusing the crown only because he feared its dangerous honour, and because he saw that true power lay in the hands of a skilful king-maker. Arnulf of Flanders was prepared for any crime; and William Longsword, the best among his rivals, was but a fickle, changeable man. To make matters worse, all these nobles were allied by ties of blood and of marriage, which seemed only to embitter the strife. Thus Gaul was the victim of a series of hateful family quarrels. Hence the endless, aimless struggle continues, and the history becomes terribly confused. Such must often be the case when the only principle followed is that of narrow self-interest, self-aggrandisement; and this, in the narrowest, most selfish sense, was the aim of one and all.

Nor were there wanting other causes of dispute. At this time, sovereigns, princes, and counts were all trying to appropriate to themselves the revenues of the rich abbeys and benefices, as Robert of Paris had done, or make them hereditary in their families. At this date the important Metropolitan See of Rheims was actually in the dominions of Herbert, and it had long been his darling object to put his son into it. Having poisoned the Archbishop, he at last gained his end; and the boy of five years old was shamefully foisted into the See, and made to lisp the responses at his institution. We have from a contemporary a naive description of the ludicrous yet shocking scene which followed these youthful consecrations, frequent at that period. The child, taught to repeat the responses or spell them if he could not get them by heart, usually behaved pitiably, sometimes breaking out into a whimper in dread of the accustomed chastisement for not knowing his lesson. For the violation of all decency Herbert's adversaries probably cared little, but they resented the dangerous increase of his power, and opposed his boy-bishop.

The quarrel continued, and Rudolf, though supported by Aquitaine, Hugh of Paris, and William Longsword, only held a precarious position till his death, 936. No sooner had this occurred than the turbulent feudatories, impatient of a master who was one of themselves, determined to have a king, and there still remained a Karoling prince to represent the royal line. Ædgifu, the wife of the unfortunate Charles, upon her husband's imprisonment, had fled with her young son hidden in a truss of hay, to the court of her brother, the great Athelstan, under whose sheltering power England became the home of all unfortunate exiles. This son, Lewis 'd'Outre-mer' (from beyond the sea), was now recalled, and, in a great council, invested with the royal authority; Hugh of Paris again refusing the proffered honour, and preferring the post of guardian to the young king. Thus, then, was the throne of France for the last time restored to the Karoling line.

In the hope of keeping some sort of thread through this miserable civil war, we have carried our sketch of it without a break to the date of Lewis d'Outre-mer's accession. We must now return and treat of the internal affairs of the duchy,

Brittany had been nominally granted to Rollo by Charles the Simple at the treaty of

Clair on Epte, but Charles in so doing had granted that over which he had no real power. The Bretons, proud of their Keltic descent, proud of having escaped the all-embracing empire of Charles the Great, resented this act. The want of unity between the various provinces had hitherto kept them quiet. They had perforce submitted to the continued devastations of the Northmen from the sea, who were seeking to carve out dependencies for themselves as Rollo had done, and to the galling yoke of the Norman duke. But now, roused by the change of rulers at Rouen, they rose under two of their princes, Berenger and Alan, massacred the Northmen in their country, and invaded the Norman duchy, William, however, completely crushed the revolt, Berenger submitted, Alan fled to the court of Athelstan, and when restored, on the intercession of the latter, was forced to accept the terms imposed by the conqueror at the first suppression of the rebellion. The result was an important increase of the Norman territory by the acquisition of the Côtentin and the Channel Islands, and the formal acknowledgment of the Norman supremacy over the rest of Brittany.

The door was thus opened to further conquests in the east and south, in Maine and Brittany. Normandy, advanced to the sea-board on the west, gained a boundary, important as well for its physical characteristics as for its two harbours; the dangerous Barfleur to the east, and the important Cherbourg to the west, marked out by the Romans as a stronghold, from whence perhaps it gained its name, Cæsaris Burgus, and now the most important port of Northern France. The district thus acquired formed the kernel of Norman nationality which sent forth in later times the conqueror of Apulia and Sicily, and many of the leaders in William the Conqueror's army.

The Channel Islands from that day forward belonged to the Norman dukes, were transferred to England at the Conquest, were retained when John lost Normandy, and to this day, though French in speech, remain English in heart and allegiance, forming distinct commonwealths dependent on the English crown, but sending no representative to Parliament, and enjoying a legislative independence perhaps unequalled by any island immediately round our coasts, if we except the Isle of Man.

We have seen how completely the followers of Rollo had thrown themselves into the dynastic quarrels of their adopted country, and assumed the language and the manners of Frenchmen. One district alone, the lately acquired district round Bayeux, formed the exception, and this now became the nucleus for the disaffected spirits. Here collected those who thought it shame to cast off their old gods, their leaders to victory, and the language which they had learnt at their mother's knee. Their connexion with the Danish part of England, the fiords of Norway, and the coasts of Denmark had apparently by no means ceased, and the new comers fostered the old Northman spirit of independence at Bayeux.

Of the amalgamation with the Franks, William Longépée was a thorough representative. Born of a Frankish mother, he had been taught to consider himself a West Frank, and had been brought up as such. Indeed, his very character, his fickleness, brilliancy, and impulsiveness, all proclaim his Frankish rather than his Norse descent, while the legend that he was, in his later days, with difficulty dissuaded from becoming a monk, shows that he had embraced Christianity with all the sincerity of which he was capable. As such he was hated by the Danish party, and the death of Rollo seemed to give them an opportunity for revolt. It is not impossible that the struggle may bear some analogy to the later dissensions in the northern kingdoms themselves. There we find Christianity supported by the kings who are aiming at centralisation and organisation, while the minor princes fight for paganism and independence. The result in Normandy was a formidable rebellion which threatened to overthrow the ducal power, and to confine the French language and religion to Evreux and Rouen. William showed for a time the greatest weakness. The terms which he had stooped to offer having been rejected, William, in despair, thought of leaving Normandy till, encouraged by the bravery of Bernard the Dane, his father's trusted adviser, with that strange changeableness which seems to have been with him a physical as well as a moral failing, he suddenly became brave as a lion, pounced on the rebels, and utterly routed them. The danger he had escaped seems to have had an important influence on William's conduct, both in internal and external affairs, and in fact to explain the inconsistencies of his later life. At first he strove to crush out the Danish party, and to become more thoroughly French than ever. Hence, perhaps, his adhesion given to Rudolf at this date, and his repudiation of the lovely Esprota, his first wife, whom he had married by Danish rite—that is, without religious ties—for Leutgarda, sister of Herbert of Vermandois, and his neglect of Richard, Esprota's son. His object then was to gain the favour of the Frankish nobles. To this we may perhaps also attribute his closer connexion with the Church, and, contrary to his usual niggardly habits, his foundation of the abbey of Jumièges. His vain attempts to gain lasting alliances in that faithless age did not succeed; nay, his own fickleness, his turn-coat policy, utterly prevented success. Thus, while he alienated the Danish party, he had not succeeded in making friends amongst his allies and relations; they hated him as the captain of the pirates, and he knew it. Therefore, just at the end of his life, we notice a sudden change of policy. A fresh incursion of Danes took place, and he welcomed their arrival and allowed them to settle peaceably in the newly acquired district of the Cotentin. His son Richard, suddenly emerging from obscurity, became the darling of his father, was entrusted to William's old tutor, Botho, the Danish-born, and Bernard the Dane, and sent to Bayeux to be instructed in the

Danish tongue. This change, we may well believe, contributed to his ruin. There had long been a bitter enmity between William and his jealous and wicked neighbour Arnulf. The two rivals had married sisters, daughters of Herbert of Vermandois, but at that time such alliances served but to embitter the strife. The Count of Flanders was not likely to look upon the nest of pirates, as they called the Normans, with a favourable eye. Already causes of jealousy had occurred. Arnulf had offered a refuge to the defeated Breton rebels ten years before, and William in revenge had aided the Count of Ponthieu whose dominions lay between Normandy and Flanders, and whose country Arnulf had coveted. Now William was allying himself with the Northmen, who were again stirring and troubling England and Gaul by their renewed incursions. They were evidently again becoming dangerous, and William, in league with Lewis, might well be preparing fresh troubles for Gaul. A dangerous coalition was arising, so Arnulf argued, and so the other princes thought, to which Lewis was perhaps lending himself, and of which William was the soul and centre. One remedy remained, a rude and decisive one: William must be murdered. Such, probably, were the main causes which led to the mysterious assassination of William. In that deed Arnulf of Arnulf no doubt was the prime mover; the actual assassin was, probably, one of the old Breton rebels who had the blood of relatives to avenge, but Hugh, at least, seems to have secretly favoured it. The plot being laid, William was treacherously invited to a negotiation with Arnulf on the Somme at Pecquigny, separated from his adherents, and basely murdered on the Flemish side of the river.

William Longsword is one of those characters whom history has falsely honoured, and he finds a place among the acknowledged heroes of France, almost among her martyrs. The fame of the Norman name, the partiality of the Norman historians who wrote for Richard his son, his tragic death, the romantic interest which surrounds the early life of his devoted son, his own attractive character, all have contributed to throw an unreal glamour round his name. In him we find the weaknesses and the strength of his double nationality. His winning, gracious manners, his ready wit and versatility, he gained from his gentle mother Popa: his bright features, his bravery, his rough sense of justice, his personal vigour, were the gifts of his father Rollo; and these earned him the love of his fellow-men. But the fair traits were shaded by darker tints. Fickleness and faithlessness, these were the faults of his mother's race and of his age, and these he shared with the rest of his contemporaries. A creature of impulse, his justice seems to have had no firmer basis than that of natural inclination. Often seriously wishing to abandon his ducal throne for the seclusion of the cloister, he yet showed scanty regard for the things of Holy Church, and was niggardly in his endowments. The monasteries were the one redeeming element in those distracted times, and these, with one exception, he carelessly neglected. The paganism of his father seems in him hardly to have been eradicated, and, following his impulse and not his conscience, he was led by circumstances from one shift to another to the fatal meeting on the banks of the Somme. Had he pursued one consistent policy and remained true to his word, he would have been at least respected, if not loved, and the wicked coalition against his life might never have been formed. As it was, he was snatched away in the midst of a changeable, aimless life; and the existence of his race and name in France was endangered by the long rule of a minor.

CHAPTER V.
THE CAPETIAN REVOLUTION.

Richard in our days would have been called a bastard, and as such he was branded even then by his enemies. He was son, not of Leutgarda of Vermandois, but of Esprota, a Breton woman of unknown lineage, whom William had previously married in Danish fashion and put away for the stately sister of Herbert of Vermandois.

These Danish marriages form a remarkable feature in Norman history. Of the five generations of Norman dukes, from Rollo to William the Bastard, or the Conqueror, the children of Richard the Good alone were born of a marriage sanctioned by the Church, and legal in our sense of the word. Loose as the marriage tie universally was at this date in Europe, we must seek for another explanation of this custom of the Normans, which found some analogy in Danish England. The Scandinavians seem to have been once a polygamous people, and perhaps this was a remnant of the ancient state of society. The position of a woman married by Danish fashion seems to have been that of a legally recognised concubine, who could not leave her husband at her will, and was recognised as his wife until he chose to sever the connexion and seek another wife. In that case the tie was dissolved, and the children were not necessarily looked upon as the legal heirs of their father. The Church would naturally defend this view and assert the superiority of the wife married according to her rites, or, as in the case of Richard the Fearless himself, enforce the subsequent celebration of religious rites between the husband and his concubine. A custom of this sort is found among the Scandinavian people of a later date, and it may have some resemblance to the custom of hand-fasting in the north of England, by which the parties bind themselves as man and wife for a year, at the end of which the connexion may be severed or finally completed at will. The so-called illegitimacy of Richard would not, perhaps, mar his claim to the dukedom in Norman or in Frankish eyes, especially since Leutgarda bore no children to his father. Still, the ambiguous position was an element of difficulty. There were enemies enough who gladly seized the opportunity of disputing Richard's inheritance; and Leutgarda, who had married Theobald of Blois, an enemy of his father, and was by some accused of having assisted in the murder, pursued her step-son all her life with the traditional hostility of a step-mother. But greater dangers surrounded the young duke. His father's death was followed by a renewed Danish invasion and settlement. The old feud between the Norman and Danish party, which had broken out in his father's time, and, though crushed, had been kept alive by his changeable policy, was revived. The Danish party welcomed the settlers. Hugh of Paris and Lewis jealously watched their opportunity. The latter, indeed, had not apparently any hand in the shameful murder of

Duke William, but the Norman power had too often endangered his throne for him to miss the chance of humbling it for ever; and Hugh had particular reasons for joining the same cause.

A few months after William's death, the sister of Otho had borne Hugh a son, Hugh Capet, the future king of France. The old king-maker had already seen his father Robert, and his brother-in-law Rudolf of Burgundy, elected kings of France. He had been the guardian of Lewis, and, although he himself had wisely refrained from aspiring to the precarious title, he now began definitely to scheme that he might be the father of a king.

Such were the threatening dangers which surrounded the young boy, and it was the successful struggle against them all which lends such romantic interest to his earlier years. The chief hope for his success, nay, for the preservation of his race, lay in two circumstances: the loyal fidelity of his father's friends, Bernard the Dane, Ivo de Belesme, and Osmund de Centvilles; and the certainty that the kingly and ducal interests of Lewis and Hugh would soon diverge and break up the coalition. For the present, however, they were firm friends. Hugh was confirmed in his dukedom of Burgundy, and the state of Normandy offered them a legitimate opportunity for interference. There, the heathen party, recruited by the renewed Danish settlement, had rapidly increased, and the young duke was either persuaded or forced to abjure his Christian religion. Thus the Christian and French parties were driven to appeal to Lewis and Hugh. The wish of some of the Danish party apparently was to unite Normandy with the kingdom of Denmark; but even short of this, the interference of Lewis and Hugh might well be justified. Rollo had sworn to become a Christian and a Frenchman, his grandson had willingly or unwillingly broken that compact, a party in the duchy had turned against their duke and appealed to them for aid; feudal ideas were fast developing, and Lewis might well claim the wardship over the fief during the minority of his vassal. Accordingly the duchy was invaded, the Danish party overthrown, Rouen seized, and Lewis gained possession of the young duke's person, while Hugh secured Evreux. United by this common robbery, Lewis and Hugh falls into the seemed firmer friends than ever; and Lewis, elated by the prospect of acquiring the whole of Normandy, granted in full sovereignty to Hugh the duchy of Burgundy, which henceforth became a dependency of the lord at Paris. But here all concord ended. Lewis wished to hold all Normandy; Hugh wished to have his share. From the very first he had been forming a party among the Normans, and now he turned against his ally. Meanwhile Lewis permanently occupied Rouen, and the young Richard, transferred to the town of Laon, remained to all intents a prisoner, where, if we may believe the Norman authorities he was treated with cruel harshness. The French party among the Normans, who had under the first impulse of terror applied to Lewis, but had no desire to become subjects of the Karoling king, felt their old spirit of independence stirred up by this base conduct. Hugh, not improbably, worked upon their discontent, and they rapidly slipped away from Lewis. Richard, aided by his trusty companion, Osmund, escaped from Laon, hidden in a truss of hay; and the standard of revolt was raised. At this moment a new ally most opportunely was found. Denmark, since the days of Gorm the Old a single powerful kingdom, was at this date in the hands of his son, Harald Blaatand (Blue-tooth), the grandfather of our Canute. In Normandy's greatest peril this honest man appeared on her coast, rallied the Normans round his standard, and meeting Lewis on the Dives utterly routed him. Lewis, made prisoner in personal combat with the hardy Danish king, escaped in the turmoil which succeeded only to fall into the hands of the enemies stirred up against him by Hugh. Harald now passed through the land, confirming the authority of the young Duke Richard and restoring the old Norman customs, and then, his mission over, returned to his northern home. Such singular disinterestedness on the part of a heathen king, if we can believe the tale, puts to shame the unfathomed faithlessness of all those so-called Christian princes with whom we have had to deal. A strange mediator between the Normans and Lewis was found in the treacherous Hugh who then became his gaoler. Deaf to the remonstrances of Edmund of England, Hugh only yielded to the threats of Otho on condition that Laon should ceded to him; and Lewis, the victim of his own greed, regained his freedom at the price of his own imperial city. Hugh and the other princes renewed their homage; but the Normans, exasperated by the treatment they had undergrone, revived their old claims to independence, and, if we may believe the partial evidence of their chroniclers, repudiated for ever the demands of the Frankish king. Still, Normandy could not hope to stand alone; an alliance was necessary, and it was sought at Paris. Self-interest alone could keep Hugh true;

but at the time this so clearly pointed to alliance with Normandy, that the Normans were justified in looking to him for aid. After all, Paris was the natural ally of the Normans. Hitherto, adhering to the oath of Rollo, they had paid a personal allegiance to the Karoling line; but now, becoming French, they of necessity turned to Paris. We have seen in the reign of William Longsword the question raised, whether they were to be Frenchmen or Scandinavians. This had been decided in favour of the former, and, therefore, French Paris, and not Frank Laon, must in future be their ally. The alliance assumed the form usual at that time. Feudal ideas were rapidly growing, and Richard, following the custom of the day, commended himself to Hugh and became his man; while Hugh, anxious to secure the friendship of the Normans for his son, betrothed his young daughter Emma to the Norman Richard.

Thus began the vassalage of the Duke of Normandy to the Duke at Paris, which, though sometimes denied by the independent Normans, was a real one, and deeply affected their future history.

We have now arrived at a point where, amid the hopeless confusion of the petty struggles, by which the kingdom had been so long distracted, two principles arise, and become definite and distinct.

Since the days of Charles the Simple the chief question at issue had been the succession to the throne of the West Franks, and the quarrels and treaties between Laon and Paris the true thread of these discontents. But till now the claim of Paris to be the sole rival of the Karoling line had been disputed by other princes. Burgundy had already given a king, and Vermandois, proud of a descent from Charles the Great, had entered the lists as a competitor. Now Burgundy was annexed to ducal Paris; Vermandois, since the death of Herbert, according to some accounts by his own hand (943), had been divided amongst his sons, while a small portion had gone to extend the ever-growing dominions of Hugh. Arnulf, since the treacherous murder of Duke William, seems to have lost influence and power. Normandy, long the chief supporter of the Karoling line, and hitherto the constant enemy of Paris, had at last commended itself to Hugh, and concluded a strict alliance. From all these causes the power of Hugh became supreme; no one arose to dispute his claim of being the leader of the opposition to Lewis and his family. The intricate plot is working out, the catastrophe is at hand, and the chief actors in that catastrophe are clearly seen.

The second principle follows from the first. We have seen that it originally was the two chief dukes of the West Franks who were allied against their king. The quarrel then was one of the ducal provincial element against the royal-imperial, two kings. Now that kingly interests were definitely at stake, it was only natural that Lewis should turn to his neighbour Otho. The king of Germany had himself to struggle against the jealousy of the rival provinces, of which many only surlily acquiesced in the establishment of the Saxon line upon the throne, and this alone would lead him to favour the appeal of Lewis. But there was another reason. Otho had probably already conceived the idea of claiming the empire for himself, and reviving in his own person the position of Charles the Great; and Lewis, too glad to get valuable aid at any price, acquiesced.

Thus, the quarrel which ensued was between two kings on one side and two dukes on the other, the provincial against the imperial element; and it was the severing of one of these alliances which really decided the question. As long as the German king supported Lewis the influence of Normandy was counterbalanced; but when that policy was temporarily abandoned by Otho, the fall of the house of Laon and the rise of Capetian France was the necessary and inevitable consequence. It is fortunate that we are able thus to clear our way, and that the main questions at issue stand out sharply, because of the details it is extremely hard to feel secure. The French and German accounts are meagre in the extreme, while the Norman overwhelm us with details which are probably semi-mythical. We shall, therefore, only briefly notice the chief points of interest.

Otho, indignant at the terms imposed upon Lewis on regaining his freedom, joined him, and their united forces invaded the territories of Hugh and Richard. Repulsed from Laon, Paris, and Rouen, they only succeeded in taking Rheims, from which they expelled Hugh's nominee, the once boy-bishop, Laon only fell in 949, and then by stratagem. The Norman chronicler Dudo and the later romancers are loud in their rejoicings over the humiliation of the kings; but though their efforts were crowned by no signal success, the cause of Lewis seems to have steadily advanced. The Church, which was again beginning to make its voice heard, declared for the kings, and Hugh was excommunicated by the Pope. The princes of Aquitaine were definitely gained over, and by

953 Hugh had made full submission. Such was the position of Lewis when he was snatched away by an untimely death at the age of thirty-three.

It has been usual to speak of the last representatives of the Karoling line as poor weakly kings, idly dreaming away their lives on the throne, or patiently submitting to become the creatures and the prisoners of their vassals; and the contrast between the strength of Charles and the incapacity of his successors has been used to point the moral of many a tale. This idea, no doubt, owes its origin to the persistency of their bad fortune, but is entirely untrue to fact. They were unsuccessful; they were, in common with the rest of their contemporaries, wanting in political morality, which often injured their cause, but they were by no means deficient in energy or natural ability. Had they been so, the line would have ended long before. The lives of Charles the Simple and of Lewis were marked by singular activity: they displayed great power of bearing up against reverses, and no mean sagacity in taking advantage of the few opportunities which presented themselves. But their lot was cast in desperate times. They were surrounded by a crowd of ambitious, turbulent, and utterly fickle feudatories, who, while they agreed in nothing else, were at one in their desire to set at naught the authority of their king, and whose faithless alliances were, perhaps, more dangerous than open hostility. Their reigns were troubled by constant incursions of the Northmen and Hungarians. The people were too much down-trodden to make their influence felt as they did at a later date, and the dynasty of Charles the Great had not been based upon the wants and wishes of the separate nationalities.

Truer is it to say, that the work would have been too much for another Charles the Great, than that his descendants were the victims of their own incapacity.

On the death of Lewis the destinies of Gaul were again in the hands of Hugh, although

Otho claimed a real but ill-defined supremacy. To the influence of these king two men we may ascribe the election of Lothaire. Otho had supported Lewis: it was natural he should support his son. As for Hugh, a king-maker he had lived and a kingmaker he wished to die; and Lothaire, at the age of thirteen, like his father before him, ascended the throne under the protection of this busy intriguing prince. Hugh, once more the guardian of his king, hastened to turn the position to his own advantage. Gaining from Lothaire a grant of the duchy of Aquitaine, he embroiled the king in a war with the princes of that country, but their combined Hugh dies forces were checked before Poictiers. The war was ended, and shortly after, Hugh's successful, restless, intriguing life was brought to a close.

Unwilling or unable to assume the crown himself, he had paved the way for his son, and this in two ways. The constant intrigues of his earlier life had his life's tended to weaken the power of the royal line, and the final alliance made with Normandy eventually served to place his son upon the throne.

Left a minor at the age of thirteen, Hugh Capet fell by the will of his father under the guardianship of Richard the Norman duke, and the alliance was cemented in 960 by the consummation of the marriage between Emma and Richard, who renewed his homage to his ward. The relations between Paris and Laon remained the same, Hugh doing homage to young Lothaire. Thus the destinies of Laon and Paris were in the hands of two boys of almost equal ages, the Karoling leaning more and more on the staff of Germany, and the Frenchman on that of Normandy. So things remained, with the exception of one short war between Lothaire and Death of Richard, until the death of Otho I.

By that event the last hope for the Karoling line was extinguished. Lothaire foolishly quarrelled with his successor, Otho II., about the possession of Lotharingia, and the war which ensued was only ended by the death of the two rivals within three years of each other.

Thus by the imprudence of Lothaire, the powerful German house was alienated at the moment when its aid was most needed.

Once more the Karoling line was chosen, and Lewis, the son of Lothaire, quietly succeeded under the protection of Duke Hugh. The one act of his reign was to alienate the powerful Archbishop of Rheims, Adalbero, whose interests were thus transferred to Paris.

At Lewis's death the crown was again referred to the will of the princes. The only two possible competitors were Charles of Lorraine, the uncle of the late king, and Hugh Capet. Of these, Charles had made himself unpopular by accepting part of Lotharingia as a fief of the empire, and had, in some sort, been already passed over when not elected to share the kingdom with Lothaire, according to the usual custom. Now that Lotharingia was definitely a fief of the Empire, Laon was evidently not the place for the capital of a French kingdom, nor the German-speaking Charles the person to be king over a French-speaking people. Indeed, when we review the past we are tempted to wonder that the Karoling line had not long ere this been abandoned, not that it was abandoned now.

But if not the Karoling line, who had better claims than Hugh? His family had already given two kings to Gaul (Eudes. 887-893; Robert, 922-923), his father's life had been one long preparation for the change, and had he willed, probably it would have occurred before. Now at least there could be no doubt. Hugh Capet could depend upon the suffrages of Burgundy which was in the hands of his brother Eudes, of the metropolitan Archbishop of Rheims, lately estranged from Lewis, and, above all, of Richard the Norman duke, who had private as well as public wrongs to avenge. There were some, indeed, who favoured Charles, but of these Aquitaine was too little connected with France to make its influence felt, and Vermandois was no longer powerful. The only influential supporters of Charles were the Archbishop of Sens and Baldwin of

Flanders; when, therefore, the Archbishop of Rheims, asserting the elective character of the crown, put the question to the vote, the election of Hugh Capet was carried by acclamation. The party of Charles, not strong enough to gain his election, took up arms in his behalf. Charles displayed the activity common to his race, and for two years carried on the struggle with considerable success, but fortune had declared against the Karolings, and now overwhelmed their last representative. Betrayed by the treachery of the Bishop of Laon, whose most sacred promise he had trusted, he and his city were handed over to Hugh. Laon ceased for ever to be a capital, and Charles remained a prisoner till his death in 1001.

The revolution which was thus consummated was one of the utmost importance to France and to Europe. Its importance, however, did not lie in the election of Hugh Capet, but in the permanence of his dynasty. The Karolings had been overthrown, and the third dynasty established by a complication of fraud, treachery, and misfortune, not by conscious adherence to any acknowledged principle. The chief actors were no doubt entirely ignorant of the important part they were playing in the history of their country. As far as they were concerned, it was little more than one phase of the petty struggles which had been for years distracting Gaul. Their motives, as before, were utterly selfish and temporary. Hugh Capet was king, as Odo his great-uncle and Robert his grandfather had been before him, but no one could tell whether his power would be more lasting than theirs; certainly no one saw the hidden forces at work which were to establish his family firmly upon the throne for full 800 years. The princes, therefore, were unconscious agents in this eventful change; for its consummation we must look to other causes.

In the accession, or rather in the permanence, of the Capetian dynasty, we see the rebound from the principles upon which Charles the Great had founded his empire. A reaction had long been operating to break up that empire; but it is not till now that its effect is thoroughly worked out as far as France is concerned. The empire had been founded upon a false attempt at unity, against which Nature herself cried out, and which had no real social or internal basis. It was a violation of all geographical boundaries—not to be lightly violated, at least in early Empire, times. The people he thus tried to unite had absolutely no common basis of nationality, no common interests, or language, or social customs, none of the bonds necessary to form a united state. It was an empire founded upon conquest, not upon the wishes of the people; an attempt to force a Teutonic government on Romanised Gaul; hence it was a purely personal rule. Nor was this all. The ideas to which it looked for strength were too complex for an early state of society. Charles had attempted to revive the old imperial ideas of Rome by the infusion of younger Teutonic ones. The Emperor of Rome, in virtue of being head of the senate, had been looked upon as the representative of the people in all things. He was high-priest as well as emperor. When Christianity was made the state religion by Constantine this position of high-priest was continued under a Christian form. Charles added to this the elective character of the German king, and the close connexion with the Church. Based on such principles as these the Empire was ill-suited to the temper of the times, and as soon as Charles's master hand was removed, the disruptive forces set to work and broke it up. The attempt to form a Christian empire was reproduced on a more modest but firmer basis by the Holy Roman Empire of Otho I. (962). In Gaul the same agencies began to move, and after a long struggle triumphed in the accession of Hugh Capet.

The natural limits of modern France are the basins of the Rhone, the Somme, the Seine, the Loire, and the Garonne, which form a network over the whole of France, now completed by her system of canals. The natural capital must be found somewhere in the centre, Orleans, or

Lyons, or Rouen might dispute the claim with Paris, but not Laon, lying as it did at the eastern extremity, on no large navigable river, close to the German frontier. The fictitious unity achieved by Charles was gradually replaced by a more real though less ambitious one, a unity defined by natural boundaries and knit together by the ties of common interest and of a common language. The Teutonic element had never really leavened Gaul. Its permanent influence is bounded by an imaginary line drawn from Cherbourg to Marseilles; west of that, fully half of France, it did not reach at all, and even east of it the Romance element soon cast off the Teutonic superstructure, broke off all connexion with Germany, and looked for a national dynasty to represent its national features. Of all the ideas upon which the Empire of Charles was based, one alone, the elective character of its king, it retained, and that a common one to European nations. Feudalism arose to complete the idea of French royalty and to fix it. The dominion of

Charles was a personal one. Against this, in France as elsewhere, was formed the idea of territorial dominion. Earlier kings had been kings of the East and West Franks, Hugh Capet was the first king of France. Thus, in every way, the dominion of the Capets was the negation of the principle upon which the Empire had been based; and this at once explains their weakness and their strength. Their power was by no means a personal one. They owed their rise to the centrifugal tendencies before which the Empire had fallen. At their accession royalty was at its lowest ebb. Their own domains were no doubt more extensive than those of the later Karolings. They consisted of Picardy, part of Champagne, the city and county of Paris, Orleans and Chartres;—a narrow strip running north and south, equally divided by the river Seine. But their power over the rest of France was probably less. South of the Loire their existence was hardly recognised, and north of it Lotharingia had been finally given up to

Germany. The connexion with Flanders was gradually weakened. The Duke of Normandy holding the very keys of their dominions and shutting them out completely from the seaboard threatened to overshadow them, while their power was further circumscribed by some hundred sovereign states, absolute within their own dominions and owing a nominal allegiance to their over-lord at Paris, which was often exchanged for an attitude of open defiance.

Whatever view we take of the character of the earlier Capetian kings—whether with some we consider them as priest-ridden weaklings, or with others declare them to be men of considerable ability and activity—we cannot but wonder how they retained the throne. They had lost the presumptive title of long possession, so valuable in earlier times. Their accession was certainly accompanied by increased power among the feudatories, with whom they were long engaged in deadly strife. Unconscious of the subtle forces which were supporting them, their lives were spent in petty struggles, until, with Lewis VI., the monarchy awoke to find that France had grown meanwhile, and firmly fixed them on the throne.

We have dwelt upon the important struggle which ended in the final triumph of Paris because the Norman dukes had been the primary agents in the revolution, and because future history. Norman history is deeply influenced by it. Since the days of Rollo, Norman history had formed an unbroken thread in the tissue of the history of France. As long as the Norman dukes remained true to the Karolings they were safe; but when Richard finally sided with Hugh of Paris, their death-knell was sounded, and it was only a question of time as to the exact moment when the event should be consummated. Thus it was the Normans who had made Gaul France, and Paris owes her position as capital of modern France above all to their agency. The effect on Normandy, on the other hand, is fully as great. Till now the Normans had been hardly accepted as Christian brethren by their neighbours; they were hated while they were feared, and branded with the name of pirates. Henceforth they gain a recognised and important position as Frenchmen. In Normandy the best French qualities appear: the vivacity, the impulsiveness, the cleverness of the Romanised Celt seem to have gained strength from the courage, the high spirit of independence, the perseverance, the chivalry of the Scandinavian. Nowhere else is the Scandinavian influence so great, nowhere else is it so permanent. Elsewhere they become rapidly lost amid the surrounding nationality, and lose their predominance; in Normandy the union of the Scandinavian nobles with the French lower classes produces a famous and peculiar type of men, the best of the French—the conquerors and wise kings of Sicily, the powerful conquerors and organisers of England, the flower of chivalry and the heroes of the Crusades. Here the *langue d'oïl* assumes its greatest polish, here rise the first of North-

French poets, here the finest of the early French cathedrals are built.

Lastly, the relations between Normandy and Paris, inaugurated by the revolution which we have been considering, deeply affected the future history of Normandy as well as that of France. Richard II. had commended himself to Hugh, the great Duke of Paris. That duchy had now grown into a kingdom. The vassalage continued, but it was due rather to Hugh Capet as duke than as king of France; and while the Capetian kings in later days ill requited the assistance they had received from their Norman vassals, the Normans were ever ready to claim their independence and reduce their vassalage to the narrowest limits.

With this Capetian revolution, in which Richard had borne so prominent a part, his public life ended, and the remaining years of his eventful reign were spent in quiet at Rouen, Nothing disturbed the internal peace of the duchy if we except a short war with England.

This is said to have been caused by the shelter offered by Richard to the

Danes, who, under Swegen, king of Denmark, and son of Harald Blaatand, were again beginning to trouble England and entering on that political conquest which culminated in the establishment of Canute upon the English throne. The war was soon put an end to through the mediation of the Pope, and is important only as forming the first instance in which the Norman dukes were brought into direct connexion with the English kings.

Richard's marriage with Emma had been unfruitful, and his children by Guenora, a woman of unknown lineage, were looked upon as illegitimate by the Church, since he had been married to her only after the Danish fashion. He now married her according to Christian rites, and, by the doctrine of the Church, his children became legitimatised. Of these Richard succeeded him, and his two daughters subsequently married Ethelred the Unready of

England and Geoffrey of Brittany. Thus, having settled the question of the succession, Richard's work was done. His reign had been a long and troubled one. Succeeding at the age of ten to his dukedom suddenly bereaved of its master by a violent death, and threatened by foes and dangers, he had successfully weathered the crisis, established the Norman family on the soil, and taken the, leading part in the change of dynasty which was so deeply to colour the future history of his race. He had outlived all his reigning contemporaries and seen a new generation arise, and yet when his long reign of fifty-three years was closed he was only sixty-three. His character is marked by all his father's best qualities without his weaknesses. Judged by the standard of to-day the morality of his private life would not stand the test, but no act of public dishonesty or faithlessness is recorded against him, and his great abilities, softened by urbanity and courtesy, gained him the love and esteem of his people. Within the duchy his reign is one of quiet seed-time and growth. Norman nobility began to arise; there are few noble houses whose lineage we can trace earlier than his reign; the feudalising process was advancing and acquiring definite form. Nor were there wanting signs of nascent prosperity among the middle classes. The Normans took readily to trade, and gladly welcomed the industrious Fleming, whose fame as a manufacturer was already known. The position of the burghers was apparently a solid one. Annual mercantile fairs existed, and Falaise was already noted for its tanneries and woollen manufactures. The latter part of Richard's reign was spent in organising his dukedom, issuing the first coinage of the Norman mint, and in restoring Fécamp and other monastic establishments which had been suffered to fall into decay during the troubled times which had preceded. In every way the Normandy of later times was arising, and, if Rollo is to be considered the first founder of the power of Danish Normandy, Richard, the last of the Danish, the first of the French Norman dukes, is the second founder of the dukedom.

CHAPTER VI.
RICHARD THE GOOD.

By the death of his father, Richard the Second, the Good, succeeded at a somewhat early age. Scarcely was he on the ducal throne when he had to meet a threatening movement on the part of the peasants. It is not often in the history of that date that we have an opportunity of judging of the condition of the lower classes. The scarcity of all written records, and the fact that the chroniclers wrote only for princes and their courtiers, have alike contributed to this. Hence, little as we know of this peasant revolt, it naturally arrests our attention. We have seen that in the days of Richard the Fearless aristocratic ideas were growing, and that the feudalising process—that is, the custom of commending oneself to an over-lord—had already commenced. Under his son these ideas increased. Brought up a thorough Frenchman, he had imbibed the aristocratic and feudal sentiments which were arising in France, and a later writer informs us that he refused to have any but gentlemen about his person, while the possessions carved out of the ducal domain for the numerous illegitimate children of the late duke increased the number of the petty lords. This, too, is the date of the rise of baronial castles. Europe probably first learnt the art of building them to protect themselves against the Northmen, the Hungarians, and Saracens, whose intermittent ravages had been common for the last two centuries; and we may be sure that the Normans would not be slow to follow the lead, and to cover the country with these defences of the strong. Hence aristocratic privilege increased, while the numerous grants made to the courtly adherents of the duke multiplied the numbers of the landlords, and brought them into close connexion with the peasantry. The peasant class in Normandy was formed chiefly of the old Romance population, who, at some time subsequent to the first settlement of the

Northmen, had fallen into the class of 'villeins' holding small plots of land for which they owed service to their superior. Elsewhere in France the condition of the lower classes was probably very wretched; they were harassed by continual war, agriculture was in its infancy, and there was no skill to struggle against adverse seasons. The increase of pestilence and famine was the sad result; forty-eight such visitations are recorded between 987 and 1057. Probably the condition of the peasants in Normandy was not so bad; a man must have bread before he can become a politician, and the peasants at this time seem to have had some ideas of self-government. To men in such a position the growth of aristocratic privilege, the multiplication of landlords, and the advance of the theory of lordship, would be peculiarly galling. This was the probable reason for the movement, which was most likely joined by some of Scandinavian descent and some small holders irritated at the growth of aristocratic privilege. Retaining perhaps from Roman times some traces of local self-government by which the decemvirs were, elected in each 'pagus' to form a municipal council, these peasants began to assemble and discuss their wrongs. The author of the 'Roman de Rou,' writing in the twelfth century, thus sums up their complaints: 'The nobles do us nought but ill, and we gain no profit from our labours. Our days are spent in toil and fatigue, our beasts are seized for dues and services, our goods wasted by continual suit's. We have no safety against our lords, and no oath is binding on them. Why should we not shake off all the evil?—are we not men as they? Dare we to do and dare: a good heart is all we want. Let us then unite, and if they should make war upon us, have we not thirty or forty hardy peasants ready to fight with club and flail to each knight? Let us only learn to resist, and we shall be free to cut our own firewood, to fish and hunt, to do our will in river, field, and wood.' Encouraged by these harangues, they deputed representatives to a general assembly, and made a 'commune,' says the same author, to talk over their common wrongs and discuss the means of resistance. The writer, a clerk of the Royal Chancery to Henry I., would not be likely to paint their motives or their actions in favourable colours. From this, an enemy's account, we may therefore fairly conclude that the movement was something more than a meaningless savage revolt against all order. We meet with no such movement' in England till the time of Richard I., when London was threatened by something of the same sort under William Fitzosbert. That was, however, only a municipal movement, confined to the city itself; and for the true counterpart of this we must wait till the rebellion of Wat Tyler in Richard the Second's reign in 1381. Like that, however, it was doomed to failure. It was looked upon as a dangerous revolt against society, and was dealt with accordingly. Richard, getting news of it before it had gained a head, crushed it out with merciless cruelty, and the chroniclers of the day recount with brutal levity how the rebels were scourged; their eyes plucked out;

their heads chopped off, and distributed as a warning amongst their neighbours. We hear no more of peasant revolts in Norman history, but it seems to have borne its fruit. When we reach the era of the written evidence, we find the villeinage of Normandy lighter than elsewhere, personal servitude did not exist, while the villein-holders of the Channel Islands seem from very early times to have enjoyed a freedom as great as that of our yeomen.

Master of his subjects at home, the Norman duke rapidly increased in power abroad. This will be best appreciated by considering the foreign relations of the duke to the various countries which surrounded him. With the German Otho he had little to do. The Normans had now become Frenchmen; and the dynastic quarrels between Germany and France, rudely settled by the accession of the Capetian dynasty, were at an end. Each country was now carrying on its work of consolidation until they should be again drawn into conflict as the age of political contests drew on.

France.

Richard the Good remained true to the policy inaugurated by his father in connecting himself closely with his over-lord the Capetian king. This policy was dictated by identity of interest. Normandy, as well as France, was surrounded by dangerous neighbours: the Duke of Burgundy, the Count of Anjou, and the Counts of Chartres and of Flanders, all of them jealous of the growing power of the two upstarts, the King of Paris and the Duke of the Normans.

The Normans had now become thoroughly French in interests and ideas, and if the Dukes of Normandy were the chief mainstay of the king, the alliance of Paris was nearly as valuable to the Norman dukes. In fact, their destinies were to advance hand in hand until their relations should be reversed by the overwhelming power of the Norman vassal.

Thus it is that in all the wars of Robert, who had now succeeded Hugh Capet, whether against Flanders or against Burgundy, we find Richard lending valuable assistance, while the

King of Paris acts as mediator in some of Richard's quarrels.

Two of these alone are of sufficient importance to be noticed.

The Burgundian Wars.

Burgundy, destined ever to be a thorn in the side of France, at this time called for the interference of Robert. The duchy of Burgundy had been secured to Henry, brother of Hugh Capet. On his death he had left it to his stepson, Otho William, a Lombard, thus violating the rights of the over-lord, the King of Paris, to whom it should have reverted. Burgundy had been too long regarded a fief of the kingdom of Paris for this to be overlooked, and Robert, gaining material assistance from Richard, asserted his claim to the fief. Otho, however, was supported by the nobles and clergy, and an obstinate war of twelve years ensued before Burgundy was restored to the Capetian king.

Otho himself subsequently gained the county of Burgundy (Franche-Comté), part of his mother's inheritance, which, with its connected territories of Alsace, Lyons, Dauphiné, and Provence, henceforth definitely belonged to the German Empire.

Eudes II. of Blois.

The dominions of Thibault of Blois, the old enemy of the Kings of Paris, were now in the hands of his grandson Eudes, second of that name. Holding Chartres, Champagne, and Brie, as well as Blois, he caused considerable apprehension to his overlord at Paris. Not content with these extensive and rich domains he seized Melun, lying on the left of the Seine, to the south-east of Paris, and important as an outpost by which his power could be restrained.

Once more Robert summoned Richard, and by his trusty aid regained this important frontier town. Subsequently, however, Richard changed his policy, and, true to the instincts of his race, which led the Normans to detect the signs of future greatness, connected himself with the rising house of Blois. Eudes married his sister Maude, and a short quarrel which ensued as to the possession of the County of Dreux, her dower, was compromised. Eudes retained possession of this important frontier signer of to the south of Normandy, and the subsequent marriage of his son Stephen to Adeliza, the daughter of Richard, cemented still closer the alliance of Normandy with that house which was eventually to give a king to England.

Nor was this the only important alliance made by Richard. With the growing power of Brittany—separated from Normandy only by the small stream of the Coesnon—he connected himself by a double marriage. He himself married Judith of Brittany, sister of Geoffrey Count of Rennes, who had established his supremacy over the country and gained the title of duke, and Haduisa his sister became Geoffrey's wife. When Geoffrey died, his sons Alan and Odo fell under the guardianship of their uncle and suzerain. Alice, another daughter, married Renaud, Count of Burgundy; while another, Eleanor, married the powerful Baldwin 'the bearded,' of Flanders.

These alliances attest the importance of the Normans abroad; but there is one more to mention, which first brought Normandy and England into close relation with one another, and was fraught with most momentous consequences to them both.

England at this date, under the incapable rule of Ethelred 'the Unready' or 'Lack-counsel,' was once more being threatened by the Danes. These Danish invasions no longer took the same character as the former inroads. The earlier were those of people driven out from their northern home, and invading England for the purpose of permanently settling in the country.

But now the three kingdoms of Norway, Sweden, and Denmark had become settled and organised, and the latter, under the powerful Swegen, was engaged in a political conquest of England. Ushered in by some piratical attacks, the Danes in the year 994 began definitely to threaten England.

Disabled by the treachery of his ealdormen, his people overawed, as all Christendom was at that time by the anticipation of the millennium, his country showing, as she ever did, the absence of a truly national spirit, the difficulties of Ethelred were great, and he was not the man to overcome them. He first resorted to the pitiful and useless expedient of buying his enemies off, and then, free from immediate apprehension, engaged in a needless war with Richard of Normandy.

We have seen before how in 991 he had quarrelled with Richard the Fearless on account of the countenance given by him to his Danish foes, and this was probably the cause of the present war. It failed, and then Ethelred, anxious to gain the alliance of the powerful Norman duke, made peace with him and married his sister Emma. This marriage, so far as Ethelred was concerned, did not serve him much. Any hopes he may have had of material assistance from his brother-in-law were misplaced. Richard had enough to do at home, and, unless he had felt inclined to engage in the war as a sort of crusade against the Northern Danes, the affair was none of his. Indeed, it is probable that the connexion of the Normans with their old kindred was too abiding to allow of this. Richard, therefore, throughout the Danish wars preserved a strict neutrality. When Ethelred was driven from his kingdom by Swegen, he offered him and his wife and children an asylum at his court, but that was all. In the brief but heroic struggle of Edmund Ironside, the son of Ethelred by a former marriage, he took no part; and when at last Canute, the son of Swegen, established his kingdom in England, he continued on friendly terms with him, and allowed Emma, the widow of the unfortunate Ethelred, to marry the usurper of his throne. Nevertheless this marriage was of the greatest importance to England. With it began the connexion of England and Normandy, which eventually led to the Norman Conquest. The sons of Emma, the Æthelings Alfred and Edward, driven from their English homes, found refuge in the Norman court, and here Edward imbibed those Norman tastes which led him to introduce Normans into England when he regained his ancestral throne. Here he contracted that friendship with William the Bastard which hurried on the downfall of his race.

Thus, then, on all sides the Norman power increased during the prosperous reign of Richard the Good. Nor is this more conspicuous in the political history of his country than in the individual energy of his subjects. We have seen the kingdom of Denmark again showing signs of warlike vigour, and again disturbing England with her invasions.

It is remarkable that Normandy itself at this date witnessed a similar movement. Hitherto the Normans had been fully employed in settling themselves in Normandy and in establishing their power in France. But now that their power was consolidated, their country became too small for their energies, perhaps unable to support the rapidly increasing population, and the old spirit of adventure and distant conquest was aroused. In fact we have arrived at the period when Normandy itself became the starting place for those expeditions which may be well said to culminate in the Norman Conquest. That, however, was undertaken by the duke himself. Those which now demand our attention were the result of individual enterprise. Spain first attracted them, and thither Roger de Toesny sailed to war against the Moors, and to found, if possible, a dominion for himself. This, however, had no lasting results. Far more important is the settlement of the Normans at Aversa in Italy.

In the eleventh century many of the Normans seem to have wandered away into Italy, partly as pilgrims to visit the sacred shrines, but ever ready to engage in any promising enterprise which might offer. Often called in by the princes of the south of Italy as mercenaries in their quarrels with one another, they finally were allowed to settle at Aversa by the Duke of Naples, and the town was built and fortified for them as an outpost against Capua.

Their character is thus described by a contemporary historian of Italy:—'The Normans are a cunning and revengeful people; eloquence and dissimulation appear to be their hereditary qualities. They can stoop to flatter; but unless they are curbed by the restraint of law they indulge the licentiousness of nature and passion, and in their eager search for wealth and dominion they despise whatever they possess and hope whatever they desire. Arms and horses, the luxury of dress, the exercises of hawking and hunting are the delight of the Normans; but on pressing occasions they can endure with incredible patience the inclemency of every climate, and the toil and abstinence of a military life.'

The condition of the south of Italy at the time was this. South of Rome lay the territories of the independent Counts of Naples and the republic of Amalfi. South of these again the Greek theme of Lombardy included all that part of the peninsula south of a line drawn from Mount Garganus to the bay of Salerno. This, recovered by Basil the Macedonian, still survived under its catapan or governor, the last remnant of the Eastern Empire,

Sicily, in the hands of the Moslem, formed part of the kingdom of Tunis, and had long been an object of desire to the Eastern Emperor. In the year 1038, Maniaces, Catapan of Lombardy, excited by the internal divisions which weakened the power of the Arabs, called in the aid of the Normans, and by their assistance regained at last the greater portion of the island. Maniaces, allies and however, by his avarice and his ingratitude, alienated his new-found allies, and a quarrel ensuing as to the division of the spoil, the Normans returned two years afterwards to avenge the injury by attacking Apulia. The Greeks were defeated in a battle on the plains of Cannae, and after two years a few towns alone remained to the Emperor of the East.

The Normans, masters of most of Apulia, organised themselves into an aristocratic republic, consisting of twelve Counts, elected by popular suffrage. Amalfi was their capital; here the Counts dwelt, and administered their affairs in military council. The president of this remarkable republic was William of Hauteville, son of one Tancred, who, with his brothers Drogo and Humphrey, had left their home in Normandy in search of foreign enterprise.

The existence of this new power raised the jealousy of both East and West. In 1049 a league was formed between the Emperor of the East, Henry III Emperor of the West, and the Pope to drive the Normans from the soil of Italy. But the Emperor of the East was called off by more imminent dangers at home, Henry III. was engaged in German affairs, and Leo IX. was left single-handed to oppose the formidable Normans with a handful of German soldiers. The Normans offered terms which were contemptuously rejected, and a battle ensued at Civitella. Here the papal squadrons were routed by the superior cavalry of the Normans, and Leo IX. himself was taken captive. The Normans had all along professed themselves to be unwilling to fight against the father of Christendom, and, now adopting the attitude of suppliants before their captive, they consented to hold Apulia as a fief of the Holy See, the Pope satisfying his scruples by the consideration that their dominions were included in the supposed gift of Constantine to the Popes of that day.

The Normans really received more than they gave. By this act of the Pope they gained a recognised position amongst the powers of Italy, and their future alliance with papal interests was dictated by sound policy.

The office of President or first Count, after having been held by William, Drogo, and Humphrey in turn, passed to Robert Guiscard (the Wise), another brother of this prolific family. The fortunes of the famous Robert Guiscard remind us somewhat of those of his more powerful but scarcely more illustrious contemporary, William the Bastard, the conqueror of England.

Conspicuous amongst his followers for his strength and grace of mien, Robert had signally distinguished himself at the battle of Civitella. In the wiles of diplomacy he was the match of the clever intriguers of the South, while his frankness and open-heartedness earned him the affection of his followers. His insatiable ambition led him to the highest flights of enterprise, in which he was checked by few feelings of justice or of humanity. Like many of his race he was avaricious and cruel; but these passions were subordinate to his lust for power, and his acts were those of the far-seeing but unscrupulous statesman marching directly to his goal, not merely prompted by wantonness. To him rather than to his brothers is due the greatness of the Normans in Italy; and while his countryman Duke William was adding the crown of England to his ducal possessions, Robert succeeded in carving out for himself a noble principality in the sunny South.

During the life of his brother Humphrey, his restless and ambitious spirit had been a cause of anxiety, and as long as Humphrey lived Robert was little better than a state prisoner. On Humphrey's death, however, the tender age of his children unfitted them for command, and Robert, gaining the suffrages of his people, was created Count of Apulia and general of the republic.

Not content with his position, he completed the conquest of Apulia and Calabria, extorted from the hands of Pope Nicholas the ducal title, and henceforth styled himself 'By the grace of God and St. Peter, Duke of Apulia, Calabria, and hereafter of Sicily.' The limits of his territory in Italy corresponded with those of the subsequent kingdom of Naples. It was composed of the Greek provinces of Calabria and Apulia, the Lombard principality of Salerno, the republic of Amalfi, and the inland dependencies of Beneventum, that city being retained by the Roman pontiff. The medical and philosophical schools of Salerno, long renowned in Italy, added lustre to his kingdom; and the trade of Amalfi, the earliest of the Italian commercial cities, extending to Africa, Arabia, India, with affiliated colonies in Constantinople, Antioch, Jerusalem, and Alexandria, enriched his ample domain. Excelling in the art of navigation, Amalfi is said to have discovered the compass. Under her Norman dukes she held the position of queen of Italian commerce, until the rise of the more famous cities of Pisa, Genoa, and Venice.

The conquest of Sicily was entrusted by Robert to Roger, his youngest brother, the twelfth son of Tancred of Hauteville, a man of like talents and ambition.

Undertaken under the auspices of the Pope, this conquest assumed the character of a crusade against the unbelievers. After a struggle of thirty years, the rich island was restored to the jurisdiction of Rome. Roger, with the title of Count, ruled as 'Prince of Sicily, hereditary and perpetual legate of the Holy

See;' and his kingdom was organised on a feudal basis.

The success of his brother furnished another spur to the ambition of Robert Guiscard. Taking advantage of a dynastic revolution at Constantinople, he and his son Bohemund commenced a series of invasions of the Eastern Empire which only ended with his death. These, though unsuccessful in their ultimate result, were influential causes of the first crusade, and deeply affected the relations of East and West for years to come.

Meanwhile in Sicily Roger had been succeeded by his son, and, in 1127, this heir of the destinies of his race added the dukedom of Apulia to that of Sicily, obtained from Pope Anacletus the title of king, and finally established the Norman kingdom of Naples. His character is thus described by a contemporary chronicler. 'He was a lover of justice and most severe avenger of crime. He abhorred lying; did everything by rule, and never promised what he did not mean to perform. He never persecuted his private enemies; and in war endeavoured on all occasions to gain his point without shedding of blood. Justice and peace were universally observed throughout his dominions.'

During his reign the intercourse between England and Sicily was close. The government was organised on principles very similar to that of England; and many an Englishman wandered south to find employment in Church and State under the Norman king of Sicily.

Under his wise rule and that of his immediate successors, the south of Italy and Sicily enjoyed a transient gleam of prosperity and happiness. Their equal and tolerant government, far surpassing anything at that day in Europe, enabled the Saracen, the Greek, and the Italian to live together in harmony elsewhere unknown. Trade and industry flourished, the manufacture of silk enriched the inhabitants, and the kingdom of Naples was at peace until she was crushed under the iron heel of a Teutonic conqueror.

CHAPTER VII.
RICHARD III. AND ROBERT THE MAGNIFICENT.

For the sake of clearness we have carried our sketch of the Normans in Italy up to the middle of the twelfth century. We must now return to the Dukes of Normandy, to trace in detail the growing connexion between England and Normandy, which was to result in the greatest conquest of all—the Norman conquest of England.

Richard II. died without a dream of the great destiny awaiting his race in the south. Three years before the settlement at Aversa, he had peacefully passed away, leaving his son Richard, the third of his name, as his successor to the dukedom. During his successful reign the dread of Normandy had increased all around. Pursuing steadily the policy of his father, he had confirmed the Capetian dynasty on the throne of France, strengthened his position by numerous alliances, and, by his quiet rule in Normandy, prepared her for her next new enterprise.

Richard III. only enjoyed his dukedom two years, and even these were clouded by domestic quarrels with his brother Robert. A dispute arose between the brothers as to Robert's share, and as to the possession of the important castle of Falaise. The reconciliation was .speedily followed by Richard's death by poison, administered, many said, by Robert.

Robert, who succeeded to the dukedom under these suspicious circumstances, has earned from the legendary writers the title of 'the devil.' How or why it is hard to say. Possibly the name is due to the hatred which surrounded the early days of his young bastard son; but it was scarcely deserved. If we except the alleged murder of his brother, of which there is considerable doubt, no evil deeds are brought against him.

Among contemporaries he was known as 'the Magnificent,' and this best accords with the reckless, extravagant liberality of his character. He bears an insignificant place in the history of Normandy, and to us is chiefly illustrious as being the father of the Conqueror. This son was the offspring of Duke Robert and Harlotta, a daughter of a tanner of Falaise, whom the duke had seen from the cliffs of Falaise and loved as she washed clothes in the neighbouring brook. The marriage ties of the Norman dukes had all been very loose from Rollo downwards. Richard II.'s children alone were born in lawful wedlock. The illegitimacy of William was therefore but a pretext; it was the humble lineage of William's mother which really excited the contempt of the haughty Norman nobles. In his very cradle the babe was cursed by William Talvas de Belesme, the descendant of Ivo de Belesme the trusty friend of Richard Sans Peur. 'Shame, shame, thrice shame,' cried he, 'for by thee and thine shall I and mine be brought to loss and dishonour.' Talvas spoke for the nobility, and several revolts were the consequence of the ill-feeling. Robert, however, triumphed over them all; and, secure at home, began to exercise that influence on the affairs of Europe which Normandy, by her position—geographical, social, and political—could not fail to wield.

Brittany—at this time under Alan, Robert's cousin—ever eager to assert her independence, attempted to throw off the homage definitely claimed since the days of William Longsword. The attempt, however, failed; Alan returned to his allegiance, and henceforth became the trusty supporter of Robert's throne.

Elsewhere the position assumed by Robert was that of a protector of exiled princes and a king-maker. Baldwin IV. of Flanders, driven forth by his rebellious son, was restored by the Norman duke. Soon after, Robert was called in to support the claim of his suzerain, Henry of France. In the year 1031, Robert of France, the life-long friend of the Norman duke, had died, leaving the crown to his eldest son Henry. His widow Constance, a woman of masculine and harsh character, disliked the retiring disposition of her elder son, and set up the claims of her spoilt youngest son Robert. The aid of Fulk of Anjou and Eudes II. of Blois was gained, and Henry, driven from his throne, was forced to throw himself on the protection of his vassal of Normandy. By his help the formidable league was overthrown, Henry was restored, and Robert his brother, contenting himself perforce with the duchy of Burgundy, became the founder of the first line of Burgundian dukes. Thus another item was added to the debt owed by the Kings of Paris to the Norman dukes. In return Henry granted to Robert the overlordship over the Vexin, a piece of border land lying between France and Normandy, and the dominions of Normandy were extended up to Versailles and St. Germain—in fact, up to the very walls of Paris.

So far Robert had been successful in all his schemes. In the next he undertook he failed indeed, but it may be said to have paved the way for the future conquest by his son. The Æthelings, Alfred and Edward, still remained exiles at the Norman court, neglected alike by

Canute, who sat upon the English throne, and by their heartless mother Emma, who had married Canute and forgotten her children by the ill-fated Ethelred.

At first Robert had continued the policy of neutrality towards England inherited from his father, and had even married Estrith, sister of Canute. Considerable obscurity surrounds the subsequent history; but according to the most probable account a quarrel ensued owing to the ill-treatment of Estrith by her husband. Robert retaliated by reviving the pretensions of the Æthelings, and claimed the cession of England to the rightful heir. Upon Canute's refusal, he attempted to invade England. Canute, however, was too firmly seated on the throne to be overthrown by this half-hearted attempt. The expedition failed, and the Dane remained in undisputed possession of his crown.

This ended Robert's political career. His life closed with a strange pilgrimage to the Holy Land, prompted by a fit of passionate remorse; for what crime, we are not told. The stories of this pilgrimage surround the name of Robert with the romance of a knight-errant. With ostentatious liberality his mules were shod with shoes of silver gilt, and carelessly attached by one nail alone that they might be lost and speak of the riches of him who had passed that way. Arrived at the court of Constantinople, he treated the Emperor with a rudeness and contempt which were best answered by the studied courtesy of the more refined monarch of the East. When he reached the gates of Jerusalem we are told of the contest of liberality between him and the Emir, Robert paying all the tolls of those pilgrims who waited outside the gates, too poor to pay their fee for entrance, which the Emir, not to be outdone, returned on his departure. On his way home Robert's pilgrimage and life were suddenly cut short in Bithynia, where he died, some said, by poison. His last act well illustrates his extravagant, senseless generosity, the predominant feature of his character, and explains the reason of his name, 'the Magnificent.'

CHAPTER VIII.
EARLIER YEARS OF WILLIAM IN NORMANDY.

We have now to trace the fortunes of one of the most remarkable men the world has, perhaps, ever seen: one of those who seem to be born to rule mankind. William the Conqueror is the best representative of the masterful Norman character. His life is one long recital of extended successful struggles against opposing forces. As a babe he had clutched the straw upon the floor and refused to release his hold, and this childish act is typical of his future life. Born to be resisted, yet fated to conquer; to excite men's jealousy and to awaken their life-long animosity, only to rise triumphant above them all, and to show to mankind the work that one man can do—one man of fixed principles and resolute will, who marks out a certain goal for himself, and will not be deterred, but marches steadily towards it with firm and ruthless step. He was a man to be feared and to be respected, but never to be loved; chosen it would seem by Providence to fulfil its resistless destiny, to upset our foregone conclusions, and, while opposing and crushing popular heroes and national sympathies, to teach us that in the progress of nations there is something required beyond popularity, something beyond mere purity and beauty of character—namely, the mind to conceive and the force of will to carry out great schemes and to reorganise the failing institutions and political life of states. Born a bastard, with no title to his dukedom but the will of his father; left a minor, with few friends and many enemies, with rival competitors at home and a jealous over-lord only too glad to see the power of his proud vassal humbled, he gradually fights his way, gains his dukedom, and overcomes competitors at an age when most of us are still under tutors and governors, extends his dominions far beyond the limits transmitted to him by his forefathers, and then leaves his native soil to seek other conquests, to win another kingdom, over which again he has no claim but the stammering will of a weak king and his own irresistible energy, and, what is still more strange, securing the moral support of the world in his aggression, and winning for himself the position of an aggrieved person recovering his just and undoubted rights. Truly, the Normans could have no better representative of their extraordinary power, and the conquest of England is well worthy of closing, as it does, the long series of brilliant acquisitions gained by strength of mind and hand and will.

In sketching the history of the man, three battles mark the three decisive epochs of ducal domination—Val-ès-Dunes, Varaville, Hastings—and under these heads we will arrange his life up to the date of the Conquest

Robert's best way to have secured the succession to his son would have been to have married the fair Harlotta. According to the opinions of those times, this would have removed the stain on William's birth, and bastard he could have been called no more. Too proud or too careless for this, Robert had satisfied himself on leaving for his pilgrimage by extorting an oath of allegiance to his bastard son from the nobles of Normandy, and entrusting him to the guardianship of his cousin, Alan of Brittany, who forgot the quarrel of a few years back and fulfilled the position of regent with honour and fidelity.

As long as Robert lived, the nobles submitted in sullen silence, but the news of his death was the signal for general anarchy. The curse of Talvas found echo throughout the limits of the dukedom, and for twelve years the life of the young Bastard was in peril.

Taking advantage of his minority and the questionable character of his title, the nobles threw off all allegiance, entrenched themselves within their fortified castles which sprang up on all sides, defied authority and harassed the country with their private quarrels and assassinations. Among the most prominent of the rebels we find Roger de Toesny, who had returned from his Spanish exploits to display the cruelties he had learnt in his warfare with the Moslem, William Talvas de Belesme, the inveterate enemy of the Bastard, and the houses of Montgomery and of Beaumont; the three last names hereafter to be well known in English history.

Alan, attempting in vain to restrain these turbulent spirits, met his death by poison before the stronghold of the Montgomeries. The other friends of the young duke fell victims by assassination, and William himself with difficulty escaped the same fate.

Hitherto the disturbances in Normandy had taken the character of isolated rebellions of individual nobles struggling for their own independence, and there had been no organised opposition to William. Over these the untiring energy of William and his few hearty advisers triumphed. Now, warned by the rapidly developing powers of William (he was by this time nineteen or twenty) that they must strike at once if they would strike at all, the nobles organised a wide-spread conspiracy. No claimants had as yet come forward to dispute the coronet with William. But now Guy, Count of Burgundy, the son of Renaud and his wife Alice, sister of Richard III., claimed the duchy as his right by birth. His appeal was readily answered by the lords of the Cotentin and the Bessin, with whom he promised to share his conquest. This part of Normandy had longest retained the memory of its Scandinavian origin, and had long ago rebelled against the French tastes and sympathies of William Longsword. But probably it was rather the hope of independence than any national antagonism which now led them to rebel, since those districts east of the Dives which Guy proposed to keep for himself sided with the young duke. Around the standard of Guy also rallied all the factious nobles who had not hitherto been humbled, and thus a formidable coalition arose. William, awakened from his sleep at Valognes by the warning cry of his court fool, 'Up, up, my lord duke; open, flee, delay is death!' with difficulty escaped an attempted surprise, and flying to the strong castle of Falaise, his birthplace, summoned the faithful to his support. His authority was acknowledged by the districts east of the Dives, and by the towns and people generally, who, we are told, even in the Bessin and the Cotentin, cursed the rebels, and in their hearts wished well to the duke.

He then appealed to his suzerain Henry. Henry had hitherto tacitly sided with the rebels, and even seized the castle of Tillières which had been built by Richard the Good to strengthen his dominions on the side of Dreux; but now dreading lest by thus supporting the revolt he might weaken his own power, he for the last time sided with the duke.

The strife which ensued took the character of a war between the semi-Scandinavian Bessin and Côtentin of the west, and the Romance element of the east, a division which, often noticeable before in the history of Normandy, was here to appear for the last time. The forces met at Val-ès-Dunes, on a broad sloping plain some miles south-east of Caen, bounded to the west by the river Orne. Here a fierce hand-to-hand encounter of mounted knights ensued. No footmen are mentioned, and the Norman archers, subsequently so famous, do not appear. On the left was marshalled the royal host against the men Dunes, of the Cotentin. On the right the Normans opposed the rebels from the Bessin. The lion Frenchmen, as they spurred their horses to the attack, raised their war-cry of 'Mont-joye Saint Denis!'—the Normans that of 'Dex aiè!'—to which the rebels answered by the names of local saints.

The struggle was long and severe. Twice was Henry unhorsed. William, more fortunate than his royal ally, here first began his successful career in arms, and struck down many a rebel knight. At last the rebels gave ground and were beaten back, then turned and fled. Many were driven by the hot pursuit of their foes into the river Orne. Here they were either drowned, or slain as they attempted to cross; and the mills, we are told, were choked by the bodies that floated down the stream. The results of this crushing defeat were decisive. Guy soon after came to terms, and retired to Burgundy. The other nobles submitted, their castles were everywhere destroyed, and William, after a struggle of twelve years, found himself at last master of Normandy. His success had been entirely due to his energy and masterly ability, and his triumph was marked by singular leniency.

But if the conduct of William after Val-es-Dunes shows that he was no man of blood, but spared when he thought it could safely be done, the other traits of his character—his extreme severity, his impatience of insult, his revengeful spirit—are clearly pourtrayed in his treatment of the rebels of Alençon.

The men of Alençon, stirred by William Talvas de Belesme, William's old enemy, in whose lordship they lay, admitted Geoffrey of Anjou into their town, and rebelled against the duke. On his approach they spread out skins over the walls and beat them, shouting, 'Hides for the tanner! plenty of work for the tanner!' in contemptuous allusion to his mother's lineage. William, angered by the gross insult, swore by 'the splendour of God' that he would deal with the mockers as with a tree whose branches are cut off with a pollarding axe; and terribly he kept his word. The town soon after fell, and William ordered thirty-two of the citizens to be brought before him. By his orders, their hands and feet were chopped off, and the dismembered limbs thrown over the castle walls as earnests of his vengeance. The garrison, pitifully craving mercy, at once capitulated, and William, having strengthened the castle, retired in triumph to Rouen.

CHAPTER IX.
FEUDAL SYSTEM AND MONASTICISM.

Leaving William secure in the possession of his ducal dominion, we must take a glance at the origin and character of the feudal system.

No question connected with the history of early institutions has been the subject of such controversy as that of the origin of this system. In the last century it was supposed to have been systematically introduced by the Franks on their first conquest of Gaul in the fifth century, as a means of governing their newly acquired possessions.

Others, while rightly allowing it to be of gradual growth, have unduly pressed the distant analogies to be found in Roman law, and have traced its development, more or less exclusively, from the forms of tenure to be found under the later Empire.

These ideas, however, have been abandoned of late, and it is now generally held to be of purely natural, that is of Frankish, growth—a gradual development of Teutonic customs, which, at most, as they acquired form, borrowed from the analogies to be found in Roman law. In tracing the origin of the institution, it will be well to consider it under its twofold aspect of a *system of land tenure,* and a *system of government.*

It had been the custom of the kings of the Merovingian House, who had ruled the Franks from the fifth to the eighth century, to grant estates to their kinsmen and followers, in return for which they exacted a pledge of fidelity. Lands so granted were termed *beneficia*; and, though perhaps originally held for life, rapidly tended to become hereditary.

In time this custom was extended by the spontaneous act of the free land-owners, who, for the sake of protection in those troubled times, surrendered their estates to some great man, or church, to be held of them as tenants by rent and service.

Thus this beneficiary system gradually became universal, and not improbably borrowed somewhat from Roman law, where the custom of holding land of another by a perpetual kind of lease, was well known under the name of emphyteusis, while the grants of lands along the frontier to friendly tribes, on the terms of military service, formed another precedent.

In this beneficiary system we have some of the elements of feudalism. The *real* relation, that is, the tie formed through the medium of land tenure, existed between landlord and tenant, and a rent was in many cases paid.

But the personal tie of vassalage was wanting. The tenant, while holding land of another, and promising to be faithful to the lord as a return for protection, was in no sense *his man*; he paid him no homage. This, the personal tie, was given by the custom of commendation, whereby the inferior put himself under the personal care of his lord. With head uncovered, with belt ungirt, his sword removed, he placed his hands, kneeling, between those of his lord, promised to become his man or vassal, and took the oath of fealty.

This vassalage had no relation to land. The tie between man and man was here a purely personal one. The vassal still might hold his land independently of his lord. He had simply, by the act of commendation, become the lord's man—had sworn to be faithful to him, and sometimes to pay him military service, the lord, on his part, engaging to defend his vassal.

It had long been the custom of the Germanic kings to collect around them a number of personal followers, under the name of the Comitatus or Gesiths; and we shall see this system in England, under its English form of thaneship, becoming universal.

Some have supposed that this happened abroad, and have traced the system of commendation from that of the Comitatus, of which they consider it a later development; others assert the independent origin of the two customs. In any case, the reason for the rise of the two systems is to be sought in the same desire of mutual protection and security; and the Teutonic institution of Comitatus, at least became merged in that of the commendation.

Here, again, the relation of the client to the patron in Roman law furnished a model from which, perhaps, something may have been borrowed.

Finally, in the union of the beneficiary tie with that of commendation, the feudal obligation arose.

Then, in every case where a beneficium was granted, or handed over by the owner to be received back again, the tie would be completed by an act of homage, and the tenant would now be bound to his lord by tenure and by fealty.

Thus society grouped itself round many centres or units. The king granted lands to his great men, who paid homage to him; they, in turn, granted out lands to those below them (subinfeudation); and all ranks tended to become connected together through the medium of land tenure.

Thus far feudalism was little more than a system of land tenure and society, and had not yet affected the machinery of government. For this we must look to the opposite process. Hitherto the movement had been a growth from below; an aggregation of inferiors round numerous superiors or centres. Now the opposite tendency comes in.

It had long been the custom of the kings to couple their grants of land with rights of independent judicature over the dwellers on that land, and, under the successors of Charles the Great, the official magistracy became hereditary. They acquired large estates, with the rights of jurisdiction; the smaller landowners gathered round them for protection, and became their vassals. Thus, as the central power lost its hold, these officials gradually established their independence, until, from the ministerial officers of the Empire, the dukes and counts became the rulers over separate principalities, with semi-royal rights of jurisdiction, coinage, and legislation, enjoying the right of waging private war, and bound to the central authority by the feudal tie alone.

By the union of these two tendencies then—the centripetal from below, the centrifugal from above—the feudal system was completed. Each held of another; all were bound to one another by obligation of service, fealty, and defence; and all eventually held of the king, the head of the feudal fabric.

Government and justice were organised on the same basis. Each separate lord had his feudal court, with jurisdiction over his immediate vassals and the tenants of his demesne. This jurisdiction varied according to the terms of grant in each particular case. Causes which the lower courts were not competent to judge were sent to the court above, and in theory the ultimate appeal belonged to the royal court.

The most important form of trial was that by combat, in which the accuser and accused appealed to God, and decided the question by the sword, but women and ecclesiastics were allowed to entrust their cause to a champion. If the combat was to settle a civil suit, the vanquished party forfeited his claim, and had to pay a fine; if he fought by proxy, the champion was condemned to lose his hand. In criminal cases, the defendant challenged his accuser or his judges, and if victorious, the punishment due to his offence was visited on them.

The lord exercised the right of levying the feudal dues upon his vassals, claimed the right of private war, enacted petty laws in the feudal court, and in some cases had even the privilege of coining money.

Besides the military tenants, who were the only proper feudal vassals, there were many others who held improper feuds on varying terms, the most usual being those who paid a fixed sum of money annually, and were exempt from all further service—free socagers.

Beneath these free tenants came the villeins, a class, perhaps, originally formed of the conquered population, but recruited in later times by many of the less fortunate who fell into this semi-servile position. These villeins were of two kinds—villeins regardant and in gross. The former held small plots of land, to which they were bound. They could not leave the land, nor could they be driven from it, but they might be transferred by their lord with the land, and had to pay him servile services by tilling the land of his demesne. The villeins in gross were little better than personal slaves, incapable of property, and destitute of redress against their lord except for the most atrocious injuries.

To the feudal system must also be traced the growth of hereditary offices. It had long been the custom for the great men to surround themselves with a multitude of dependents, who filled offices which now would be considered menial, but then were looked upon as honourable. In feudal times these offices became hereditary, and thus we find the titles of steward, seneschal, marshal, chamberlain, and butler held as inheritable offices by great families under the greater feudal lords.

The essential principle of feudalism was that of mutual support and fidelity. The lord promised to protect and do justice to his vassal, the vassal to be faithful and do service to his lord. If the lord omitted to fulfil his part of the contract, the vassal might abandon his allegiance. If the vassal neglected his duties, his land would forfeit to the lord.

The duties of the vassal were briefly these. He had to do 'suit and service' to his lord's court. Of this court he was one of the judges, and if himself accused, would enjoy the right of trial by his peers. He had to serve his lord for forty days when required, and go into captivity for him as hostage when taken prisoner, service. Further, he was subject to the following incidents.

On succeeding to his estate he had to pay a fine under the name of a relief.

He had to contribute towards the dower of his lord's eldest daughter, towards the expenses incurred in knighting his eldest son, and to the ransom for his lord if taken captive.

The lord had in some cases the right to wardship of the estate of his tenants during the minority of the heir, and could marry his ward to his own nominee or exact a fine on refusal.

Closely connected with feudalism the institution of knighthood or chivalry grew up. This is probably to be traced to the primitive Teutonic custom of investing the youth arrived at man's estate with his arms in the full assembly of the tribe. In feudal times the ceremony would be performed in the castle of the lord, and would be conferred not only on his own sons, but upon the sons of his vassals, whereby another bond was formed between the lord and his dependents. Any knight, however, might in theory confer the dignity.

By the Church the ceremony was invested with a semi-religious character, especially during the crusading period. The would-be knight, after bathing in a bath as if to wash away his sins, was robed in a symbolical garb, and left within the church to pass the night in prayer and meditation. Next morning, after confession and reception of the Eucharist, he went to his initiation. His arms and spurs were buckled on him by knights or ladies, and, kneeling before his lord, he received the accolade, or three blows across the shoulders with the flat of the sword. Then swearing to serve God faithfully and fight for His faith, to maintain the right of the weak, especially of women, to be honest in all his dealings, and to be true and loyal to his lord, he rose a knight.

The systematic establishment of this form of society and government seems to have been confined to the limits of the Empire of Charles the Great—that is, to Germany, France, Arragon, and Italy. In the last, owing to her after history, it was not of lasting influence, except in the Norman kingdom of Sicily; and though it was subsequently transferred to England by the Normans, whence it spread to Scotland, it there appeared, as we shall see, in a modified and exceptional form. Within these limits the influence of the feudal idea was supreme. Not only did it affect the tenure of land and the framework of justice and government; it threw its all-embracing arms over the Church itself. The bishops held the lands of their sees by feudal tenure, and paid homage for them, and hence, as we shall see, arose the quarrel about investitures. The papacy, under Gregory VII., adopted the same phraseology and shape, became a spiritual monarchy after the feudal type, and aspired to be the feudal superior of Western Europe, to whose suzerainty the kings and the emperor himself should be subject.

Its effect upon society must now be noticed. Rising as it did out of the circumstances and wants of the times, it had a meaning and did something towards the development of the individual and of society. The attempt at centralisation introduced by Charles the Great had been premature, and, in the disorganised state of society which followed, fell to ruin. Here feudalism came in, and by its decentralising influence helped to develope local institutions and self-government.

At the same time, the tie which in theory existed between all members of the system, weak though it was, yet kept France in some sort together, and prevented the rise of independent kingdoms, as was the case in the Eastern empires.

In the right of the vassal to defy the lord lay the germ of the future right of resistance to arbitrary rule; and since in theory no suzerain could exact other than the customary dues, or pass laws without his vassals consent, who in turn was held to represent his sub-vassals, the idea of popular assent to taxation and legislation was maintained.

To it again we owe the growth of territorial as contrasted with personal power. Nobility, which had hitherto been purely a personal honour, became territorial. The dukes, counts, and barons assumed titles from their castles or domains. They became the lords of the land over which they ruled, and by virtue of their position as owners of the land enjoyed rights of jurisdiction over their vassals. The kings followed suit; once the personal kings over their tribes, they now became the over-lords of all the land occupied by their tribes, and the kings of the territory by that right. Hence the final change to territorial from personal sovereignty. Moreover, the hereditary principle thereby perfected was necessary to real advance, since without it progress was dependent upon single lives, and continuity difficult to maintain. Meanwhile, within certain limits, something was done towards the development of individual character. This will be best appreciated if we recall the character of feudal life. Imagine a castle perched on some rock or cliff detached from the mountains near, with a river flowing at its feet. The rock is difficult of access, and nature has been assisted by the work of man. Strong walls surround the castle. The gates are guarded by heavy doors, and every approach commanded by narrow mullioned windows, from which arrows and other missiles may be shot. Enter the gates and you find yourself in a small courtyard laid down with turf. Within, the castle is dark and weird, lit by straggling sunbeams which pierce the narrow windows. The dungeon and the cellars are beneath; the hall and sleeping-rooms above. The hall alone looks cheerful. Here at least there is some space, some light. A huge fire crackles on the hearth, and here the lord and his family pass the days, here the jongleur or bard sings his lays, and here the feudal feasts are held. The lord may go forth to the war or the chase, but his family, for the most part, stay at home; and in the long winter evenings, or in times of danger when the castle is tightly closed, he and his family are necessarily thrown together.

The castle is also tenanted by his retainers of varying rank. His vassals' sons come hereto learn their knightly duties and the use of their weapons with the children of their lord. The seneschal, the marshal, the chamberlain, the butler, men of honourable birth, complete the circle within the walls. At the foot of the castle lie the humble homesteads of the villeins, and hard by perhaps the feudal chase, where the lord preserves the deer with loving care and leads forth his retainers to the hunt. We can now understand the effect of such a life upon the character of its inmates.

By it the ties of domestic life were intensified. The lord, living as he did within the castle, surrounded by his wife, his children, and his retainers, was drawn close to them. He learnt to look upon his children, especially his eldest son, as the inheritors of his name and power, and therefore to take a pride in them; while the children, accustomed to their father's presence, learnt to love and to obey. The position of the wife, as mistress of the castle in her lord's absence, was raised, she acquired dignity and commanded respect while her influence over her children was beneficially exercised. Thus in every way domestic virtues were advanced. To this end chivalry also tended. With much exaggeration and folly, at least it fostered the principles of honour and of justice, formed a school of moral discipline, and indirectly improved the position of women, whose cause every knight swore at his initiation to support. Hence poetry and romance took form. These, while they threw a false splendour around the feudal character, and obscured the glaring inconsistencies, the misery which surrounded the feudal castle, at least paved the way for literary and artistic refinement. Lastly, to the relations which existed between the lord and his retainers may be traced the origin of the principle of loyalty.

Such were some of the benefits which society owes to feudalism. But their influence was often weak and intermittent, and they were sadly marred by glaring defects. The tie which bound the vassal to his lord was ever weak, and the religious bond once gone, isolation set in. Every feudal noble who could build a castle shut himself within its walls, and defied his neighbours and his over-lord. Living an idle, useless life, he found excitement only in the chase or in wild, reckless adventure. Hence society was sacrificed to the individual. The disruptive tendencies became predominant. Feurdal independence arose and developed into anarchy, and a state of chronic warfare ensued which we have so often seen illustrated in the history of Normandy.

Meanwhile the gulf between classes became wider. It was the object of every feudal lord to gain independence from his suzerain, and then to crush out all beneath him. Before them the lesser nobles fell, and tyranny increased. Amidst this selfish struggle of the nobles, the interest of the lower classes was neglected. They never had found any real place within the narrow circle of feudalism. Its humanising influence stopped at the knight, and the villein was scarce regarded as a fellow Christian. In early times perhaps his condition, though servile, was bearable, but as the isolation between classes and aristocratic pride advanced, it rapidly grew worse. The gulf between the military and non-military classes, a term synonymous with noble and ignoble, grew wider every day, and justice became the right of the strongest. The continual anarchy which prevailed added to their misery. While the noble shut himself up in his castle, his villeins fell a victim to his enemies, and saw their lands and homes harried by a cruel, ruthless soldiery. Now and then the villeins rose, as in the famous insurrection of the peasants (997), only to find that the nobles, generally so disunited, were at one in their determination to crush out their liberties and to reduce them to abject slavery. Against this senseless strife and class isolation the Church protested feebly. Here and there a town arose and extorted privileges from its lord; but for the lower classes, and for any further advance, the only hope lay in the establishment of royal power, and the subjection of these petty tyrannies to the despotism of one.

How far feudalism was at this date established in Normandy it is impossible, in the absence of all contemporary evidence, to say. When Rollo invaded Normandy the feudalising process had already begun, and in the relations which existed between the Norman dukes and the Karolings or Capetian kings, respectively, we see evident traces of the feudal idea. But the dependence of Normandy on Paris was never great, and Norman pride was continually displayed in assertions that her dukes held Normandy of 'none higher sovereign in chief but of God.'

The introduction of feudal government within the duchy has been ascribed to Richard the Fearless; perhaps it was not perfected until after the conquest of England. All that we know of the government of Normandy, anterior to that date, has thus been briefly summed up: 'The duke ruled as a personal sovereign with the advice of a council of great men. Under him were a number of barons, who owed their position to the possession of land for which they were under feudal obligations to him, and which they took every opportunity of discarding.' Their nobility was derived partly from Norse descent, partly from connexion with the ducal family, to which most of them were related, and they were thus kept faithful, partly by a sense of interest, partly by the strong hand of their master. The population of cultivators lived under the aristocracy—Gallic in extraction, Frank in law and custom, and speaking the Romance language which had been created by their early history. These were in strict dependence on their lords, though with some faint remembrance of the comparative freedom which they had enjoyed under the Frank empire, and perhaps enjoyed greater privileges than their equals elsewhere in France, while within the towns some commercial prosperity and a strong commercial feeling subsisted which broke forth now and then, as in the city of Le Mans, 1073.

Nothing but the personal character of the duke prevented the territory thus lightly held from dismemberment. The strong hand had gathered all the great fiefs into the hands of kinsmen whose fidelity was secured by the right of the duke to garrison their castles, and whose tyrannies were limited by the right of the duke to enforce his own peace. Their attempts at independence led to continual quarrels, and were checked by ruthless bloodshed.

In the history of Normandy during the early life of William, we see the two conflicting principles well illustrated which at that time divided Europe, and in later days were once to be united in the crusades. On the one hand there was the love of excitement and adventure, often degenerating into ferocity, fostered by feudalism itself, which led to expeditions to foreign lands in search of plunder and fresh conquest, or found a worse outlet in promoting anarchy at home. On the other, there was the strong religious enthusiasm, which, now that the dread of the millennium had passed, took shape in renewed activity. Hence the increasing passion for pilgrimages to the Holy Land; hence the proclamation of the 'Truce of God,'—an attempt to check the anarchy and rapine of private war by the terrors of ecclesiastical censure. By this, at first, all private war whatsoever was forbidden; but subsequently, as published in Normandy, the prohibition was limited to half the week. From the evening of Wednesday to the morning of Monday, no violence of any kind was allowed; the days of Christ's Supper, Passion, and Resurrection, were at least to be kept from bloodshed.

Not the least important outcome of the religious enthusiasm of the day is to be found in the great revival of the Benedictine rule, and the accompanying rapid growth of monasteries and perfection of architecture in Normandy. 'It seemed,' says an old chronicler, 'as if the world were awakening, and, casting off its ancient rags, were clothing increase of itself anew in a white robe of churches.' monasteries When first the Northern pirates invaded Gaul, churches and monasteries had been alike destroyed; under Rollo's descendants these ravages were repaired, and the dukes of Normandy became the most beneficent patrons of ecclesiastical foundations. The famous house of Jumièges, which Hasting the pirate had destroyed, had been restored by William Longsword; Fécamp and Mont St. Michel owed their foundation to Richard the Fearless; and, under Richard the Good, who himself was a great restorer, the movement spread to the nobles. It soon became the custom of every great lord to have a monastery on his domain. Thus Normandy grew to be the richest country in the world for ecclesiastical foundations, and the home of the rising Gothic architecture, which, borrowed from the southern plains of Lombardy, here reached its most vigorous growth. William himself, during his later years in Normandy, founded two abbeys at Caen, and showed himself a munificent patron of ecclesiastical foundations. Yet the most important foundation at that time, that of Bec, was not due to the patronage of the great, but to the individual energy and devotion of a simple knight.

Herluin had in early life been a vassal of Count Gilbert of Brionne, and a prominent actor in the clannish quarrels of the time. Wearied of the secular life, he at last refused to execute some service for his lord which he thought unjust. In revenge, the Count ravaged his lands and those of his tenants. Herluin, summoned to his lord's court, only pleaded for his poor tenants, and demanded nothing for himself. When asked what he really wished, 'By loving this world,' said he, 'and by obeying man, I have hitherto much neglected God and myself. I have been altogether intent on training my body, and I have gained no education for my soul. If I have ever deserved well of thee, let me pass what remains of life in a monastery. Let me keep thy love, and with me give to God what I had of thee.' The Count, touched by his words, granted him his wish. Herluin, receiving ordination, retired to the wild neighbourhood of Brionne, collected a devoted band of men, who, like himself, were flying from the world, and finally built his monastery upon the banks of a beck in the valley of Brionne, near the forest of that name. The cloister, at first of wood, was destroyed by a storm. This, attributed to the malicious enmity of Satan, did not cast down the energy of the monks of Bec. Again they set to work, and built it this time of stone.

Such were the small beginnings of Bec, founded on the Benedictine form. Herluin himself had not learnt to read till at the age of forty, and his monks were illiterate men. Thus Bec might have remained, an obscure and humble monastery, but for the accidental arrival of a stranger who changed its fortunes and its history. Lanfranc, a native of Pavia, had gained great renown as a student of civil law in that university, then famous for her imperial leanings and her schools of Roman law. Attracted, perhaps, by the fame of the Norman name, he wandered across the Alps and founded a school at Avranches in the Côtentin.

This journey of Lanfranc may serve to illustrate the all-embracing character of Norman civilisation, which for years attracted the best minds of Europe. Hitherto Lanfranc's learning had been wholly secular, but now he fell under the influence of the religious movement in Normandy. Seized one day by lawless men on his way to Rouen, he was robbed, and left bound to a tree in the forest near the monastery of Bec. Night came on and he tried to pray, but no psalm or office rose to his lips. 'Lord,' he cried, 'I have spent all this time and worn out body and mind in learning, and now, when I ought to praise Thee I can remember nothing. Deliver me from my need, and with Thy help I will so correct and frame my life that henceforth I may serve Thee.' Released next morning by some passers-by, he asked the way to the humblest monastery near, and was directed to Bec. There, prostrating himself before Herluin, he begged to be received as a monk, and accepted the rigorous discipline of his rule.

The monastery of Herluin, founded after the most severe model of St. Benedict, had no place for learning. Worship and prayer, work and meditation, were alone allowed; but Herluin soon found that this would not suit the mind of Lanfranc, and by his leave Lanfranc began to teach. People soon flocked to hear his lectures;

he rapidly rose to the position of prior, and under him Bec became the most famous school in Christendom, and one of the intellectual centres of Europe. 'Under Lanfranc,' says a chronicler, 'the Normans first fathomed the art of letters, for under the six dukes of Normandy scarce anyone among the Normans applied himself to liberal studies, nor was there any teaching found till God, the provider of all things, brought Lanfranc to Normandy.'

Lanfranc had come to Bec a scholar of civil law, but he then abandoned all secular studies and devoted himself to theology; as prior of Bec, he became a prominent theologian, and stood forth the champion of the Church in her controversy with Berengarius on the doctrine of the Eucharist.

From this day forth Bec became the foremost of Norman monasteries, and counted among her children three archbishops of Canterbury.

The monasteries of that date formed the most important social machinery of the times. The monks were the best agriculturists of the day, and the pioneers of civilisation. Settling in some unreclaimed spot, they made a clearing of the forest, tilled the lands, whilst their monastery formed a nucleus round which the farmers might settle. It thus became the school for the children, the hospital for the sick, the almshouse for the poor, the inn for the traveller. Nor was this all. Here alone were any remains of the ancient classics or Latin fathers preserved; here alone the pursuits of learning and of the finer arts were followed. Here church music, the writing and illumination of missals, bell-founding, organ-building were pursued. Here, lastly, lived the chroniclers to whom we are indebted for nearly all that we know of those days. It was chiefly through their agency that such literary intercourse as then existed was maintained. In the absence of printing, and owing to the scarcity of manuscripts, the only way of acquiring knowledge was by sitting at the feet of some great scholar. Hence aspirants after learning wandered over Europe, from monastery to monastery, or school to school, and Europe was drawn together. It was thence that all the great movements for regenerating society and the Church came.

CHAPTER X.
REVIEW OF ENGLISH HISTORY.

While William had been successfully struggling with his enemies in Normandy, and developing those powers of body and mind which were hereafter to nerve him to greater deeds, events had occurred in England of the nearest interest to himself.

We left England under the strong hand of Canute the Dane, and noticed the failure of the attempted restoration of the Æthelings by Robert the Magnificent. The aim of Canute had been to found a great Anglo-Scandinavian kingdom of Denmark, Sweden, Norway, and England. King nominally of four kingdoms and actually of three—England, Norway (won from St. Olaf),' Denmark, and half Sweden—he assumed an imperial position and looked upon himself as Emperor of the North. The Eider was the boundary of his empire; his daughter Gunhild was betrothed to the Emperor Henry

III.; and the Danish chroniclers loved to speak of the three great empires which divided the world—the German, the Scandinavian, and the Greek. Of this empire Northern England was to be the centre. Here Canute wished to make his home, while he ruled his dependencies through dependent kings.

As soon as he was firmly established on the English throne, and when those traitors who had contributed to his success, but whom he rightly never trusted, had been overthrown, his policy, at first ruthlessly severe, entirely changed. He now became, in spite of a few contradictions of character, a just and liberal monarch; and his subjects, forgetting his title by conquest, looked upon him as their freely-chosen king. In this he is a fair type of his people, who now, as at other times, rapidly amalgamated with their conquered subjects, and adopted their more advanced civilisation.

Trusting to the fidelity of the English, he dismissed all his soldiers except a few body-guards, married the Norman Emma, the widow of their late king Ethelred, and looked to the prosperity of his country and the love of his people as the best defence against the surprise of treachery. In his legislation, while he allowed a separate political existence to the North and South—in the North the Danish law obtaining, in the South the English—no difference was made between Dane and Englishman. The Church had been the centre of national resistance to the Dane, yet Canute allied himself closely with it; sided with the monastic party, the party of real advance at that time; respected the English saints; enforced the payment of Peter's Pence to Rome; and was himself a liberal benefactor to ecclesiastical institutions.

But his empire, as such empires in early days must be, was a purely personal one, and on his death it fell again into its natural divisions. Norway, which Canute had left to his son Swegen, soon returned to Magnus, the representative of its old kings, and Denmark, left to Harthacnut, passed to another distant branch.

Meanwhile in England the love which Canute had inspired by his wise and conciliatory rule was dissipated by the bad government of his sons, Harold and Harthacnut, who ruled in turn. After seven years of misgovernment, or rather anarchy, England, freed from the hated rule of Harthacnut by his death, returned to its old line of kings, and 'all folk chose Edward to king,' as was his right by birth. Not that he was, according to our ideas, the direct heir, since Edward, the son of Edmund Ironside, still lived, an exile in Hungary. But the Saxons, by choosing Edward the Confessor, re-asserted for the last time their right to elect that one of the hereditary line who was most available.

With the reign of Edward the Confessor the Norman Conquest really began. We have seen the connexion between England and Normandy begun by the marriage of Ethelred the Unready to Emma the daughter of Richard the Fearless, and cemented by the refuge offered to the English exiles in the court of the Norman duke. Edward himself had long found a home there in Canute's time; the attempt to restore him and his brother has been already mentioned, and after Canute's death another attempt, probably abetted by Duke William, had ended in the death of Alfred and the narrow escape of Edward himself. Thus brought up under Norman influence, Edward had contracted the ideas and sympathies of his adopted home. On his election to the English throne the French tongue became the language of the court, Norman favourites followed in his train, to be foisted into important offices of State and Church, and thus inaugurate that Normanising policy which was to draw on the Norman Conquest. Had it not been for this, William would never have had any claim on England, the question of Edward's will and Harold's promise would never have vexed the historian, and, as far as we can see, the interests of England and Normandy would have been indefinitely separated. To understand, therefore, the Norman Conquest aright, we must consider the reign of Edward as its Conquest, prelude, the gradual gathering of the forces which were subsequently to dispute the kingdom on the field of Hastings, and the quarrels between the Normanising and English parties as the skirmishes which preceded the final action. Viewed in this way alone is the reign of Edward the Confessor seen in its true perspective; the apparently meaningless quarrels which characterise it assume their true importance, and the interest, otherwise disjointed, centres round the two opposing parties.

Of these parties the two representatives are Edward the Confessor and Godwine, succeeded by his son Harold, and their quarrels will give us the natural divisions of the reign.

Of all Canute's schemes one, and that his most mistaken one, alone seems to have left any definite trace. Under him England had been divided into four great earldoms—

Northumbria, Mercia, East Anglia, and Wessex. This was clearly to perpetuate her want of unity and nationality, a fruitful cause of England's weakness; and the jealousies of these rival houses now endangered her prosperity and paved the way for the Norman Conquest.

To the north of the Humber, Northumbria was now in the hands of Siward the Dane, and, true to its Danish memories, was more independent than any other part of England, though still nominally subject to Edward the king.

In the centre of England, Leofric and his wife Lady Godiva held the old division of Mercia, and bestowed their riches with boundless liberality on ecclesiastical foundations.

In the south, Godwine ruled the old kingdom of Wessex: while his son Harold held East Anglia.

Edward, raised to the throne chiefly through the influence of Godwine, shortly married his daughter, and at first ruled England leaning on the assistance, and almost overshadowed by the power of the great earl. But this ill-matched union was not based upon real identity of interest, and there could be little sympathy between them. One was the stout Englishman who looked with jealousy on the foreigners pouring into England and holding the highest offices of state and church, whose cry was 'England for the English,' and who might have said in the words of a future assertor of English policy against the foreign-hearted Henry III., in many ways the antitype of Edward, 'Sir king, we tell you that the policy of the foreigners is both dangerous to yourself and fatal to the realm. These foreigners hate the English, and when they assert their rights call them traitors.' The other was the weakly king, who, careless of the ultimate results of his policy, was following his foolish personal impulse, and calling in foreigners to sow discord in his realm.

Already Robert of Jumièges, a Norman, had been advanced to the See of Canterbury; while Raoul the Staller, and a host of other foreigners, surrounded Edward in his court, and threatened to deprive the English of their just rights as ministers of their king. The old suspicion was now again revived by Robert of Jumièges, 'who did beat into the king's head' how likely it was that his brother had come to his death through Earl Godwine, Plainly there was cause and plenty for the gradual estrangement which took place between them.

A quarrel brought matters to a crisis. Eustace, Count of Boulogne, a foreigner, but brother-in-law of the king, as he returned from a visit to the court, demanded lodgings for his retinue of the city of Dover. The burghers remonstrated, blows ensued, and the Frenchmen were driven with shame and loss from the town. Eustace forthwith went back to his brother-in-law and demanded vengeance for the insult. Godwine was ordered, as Earl of Wessex, to punish the rebellious townsmen of Dover. He refused, claimed a legal trial for the citizens, and demanded that the foreigners should be expelled the country.

Upon this the king, supported by Earls Leofric and Siward, who were jealous of the growing family of Godwine, revived the charge of the murder of the Ætheling Alfred against him, and banishing him and his sons, obtained a sentence of outlawry against them. Godwine, obliged to bow before the united power of his enemies, was forced to fly the land. He went to Flanders with his son Swegen, while Harold and Leofwine went to Ireland, to be well received by Dermot, king of Leinster. Many Englishmen seem to have followed him in his exile: for a year the foreign party was triumphant, and the first stage of the Norman Conquest complete.

It was at this important crisis that William, secure at home, visited his cousin Edward. He had not hitherto taken any part in the affairs of England. He had been too closely employed in establishing his own authority to look abroad, and the accession of Edward had taken place without any aid of his. But friendly relations we may be sure had existed between the two cousins, and if, as is not improbable, William had begun to hope that he might some day succeed to the English throne, what more favourable opportunity for a visit could have been found?

Edward had lost all hopes of ever having any children. Edward the Ætheling, the direct heir as son of Edmund Ironsides, was far away in Hungary, and now the English party had been overthrown, and the Norman party triumphed. William came, and, it would seem, gained all that he desired. For this most probably was the date of some promise on Edward's part that William should succeed him on his death. The whole question is beset with difficulties. The Norman chroniclers alone mention it, and give no dates. Edward had no right to will away his crown, the disposition of which lay with King and Witenagemot (or assembly of Wise Men, the grandees of the country), and his last act was to reverse the promise, if ever given, in favour of Harold, Godwine's son. But were it not for some such promise it is hard to see how

William could have subsequently made the Normans and the world believe in the sacredness of his claim; and it was not unlike the character of Edward to follow the temporary impulse of his feelings, then full set against the family of Godwine, and to promise the crown to William, the best representative of those Norman tastes and ideas which he loved so well.

William returned to Normandy; but next year Edward was forced to change his policy, and the attempt of the French party to win England for their own was found to be premature. The English sympathies of the people were too strongly rooted to endure the exile of Godwine, the representative of their party, and the king; deaf for a time to the petitions from Henry I. of France and Baldwin of Flanders in favour of the great earl, was forced by the successful expedition of Godwine and the seizure of London, which declared for him, to submit to his return.

A reconciliation followed, when Godwine solemnly cleared himself, by oath in a public assembly, of any complicity in the death of the young Alfred.

The English party thus once more triumphant, a general flight of foreigners ensued. Robert of Jumièges, the Norman Archbishop of Canterbury, the leader of the Norman favourites, in haste quitted his See and the soil of England, says the Anglo-Saxon Chronicle, 'leaving behind him his pall and all his Christendom here in the land, even as God willed it, because he had taken upon him that worship as God willed it not,' and was deposed from his primacy 'because he had done most to cause strife between Earl Godwine and the king.' He was succeeded in the primacy by the Anglo-Saxon Stigand, once the chaplain of Queen Emma. The party of Godwine once more ruled supreme, and no mention was made of the gift of the crown to William. Godwine, indeed, did not long survive his restoration, but dying the year after, 1053, left his son Harold Earl of the West-Saxons, and the most important man in England.

CHAPTER XI.
LATER YEARS OF WILLIAM IN NORMANDY.

William, warned by the experience of his own early life, had for some time been eager to find a wife who should bear him an heir. This was not of more importance to William than to Normandy itself. There was, indeed, no illegitimate son to succeed his father or to dispute the claim with a legitimate son, for William, in a profligate age, was severely pure. But the absence of a lawful heir meant nothing but a repetition of anarchy at his death.

His choice had fallen on Matilda, daughter of Baldwin de Lisle, Count of Flanders, and a better choice could not have been made. The Counts of Flanders assumed at that time almost a princely position. They could count among their ancestors on the spindle side the Kings of Wessex, Italy, and Burgundy, and even claimed descent from Charles the Great himself. Their position as Counts of the borderland between France and Germany, stretching from Calais almost to the Rhine, made them peers of the Empire and of France, and assured them a most important position in either country.

To William the alliance of Flanders, divided as it was from Normandy only by the narrow strip of Ponthieu and Boulogne, would be most valuable, and the direct descent of Matilda on the mother's side from Alfred of England himself, might be thought to add to William's future claim, on England.

The duke's interest clearly pointed to the marriage, and this, as well as his genuine love for Matilda, must explain the tenacity with which he clung to it. One obstacle, however, stood in his way. The Pope, on some grounds of consanguinity, forbad the marriage. It is not clear what those grounds were, but the prerogative claimed by the Pope in such matters was very wide, and it was on the whole accepted by the moral consent of Europe.

William, however, would not be thwarted, and, after a fruitless attempt to gain the papal dispensation, he wedded his bride in the teeth of papal threats. Then, however, an unlooked-for opponent arose. Lanfranc, Prior of Bec, denounced the marriage.

This was the first introduction of William to one whose future history is so closely woven with his own. William, irritated at this new-found opponent, ordered the granges of the abbey to be fired, and Lanfranc to quit the duchy. But here the wit of Lanfranc stood him in good stead. Overtaken by the duke on a lame horse, he bade him see how implicitly his commands were being obeyed, and 'Give me a better horse,' he said, 'and I shall go the speedier.' The duke, with a laughing reply that he was the first criminal who had dared to ask a boon of him, stopped the fugitive; Lanfranc gained the opportunity he desired or speaking personally with the duke, promised to support his cause, and soon after obtained the papal dispensation. From that moment he became his most trusted counsellor both in church and state.

We have dwelt somewhat in detail on the circumstances of this eventful marriage, because it was the cause of the friendship of these two men, a friendship fraught with momentous consequences. Also because the marriage itself marks a definite step in William's career. By it the ancient hostility between Normandy and Flanders, born of the murder of William Longsword by Count Arnulf, was fairly laid. The duke's position was strengthened by a powerful alliance, a link was added to his claim on England, and that bond was begun between Flanders and the future conqueror of England which was hereafter to be drawn closer by the commercial interests of the two countries, and to be productive of great results in the history of our island.

We have now come to an important crisis in the relations between Normandy and France. Since the days of Richard the Fearless, an alliance of the strictest kind had existed between the dukes and their over-lord at Paris—an alliance founded upon mutual interests. By the help of the Capetian kings, the Dukes of Normandy had risen to be the first peers of France, while to the Duke of Normandy the Kings of Paris had owed their throne, and the establishment of their authority against their neighbouring foes. Henry himself had gained his crown against his brother Robert chiefly through the influence of Robert the Devil, and hitherto, except for a brief period during the minority of the duke, had requited that assistance by supporting William.

But now their interests split, and henceforth this friendship is changed for the most bitter hostility. The reason is not far to seek. The Duke of Normandy had become too powerful. Master of a rich and fertile country running from the County of Ponthieu to the confines of Brittany, and from the sea to the very gates of Paris, they held the keys of royal France. They shut the king out from all hopes of advancing to the sea-coast, and commanded the mouth of the

Seine river on which Paris stood. They were over-lords of Brittany, and closely allied by ties of marriage with that country as well as with Flanders and Ponthieu. Even in later days, when the Kings of Paris ruled over most of the present France, Normandy, in wealth and importance, though not in extent, formed a third part of the kingdom in which it was merged. From this we may judge of the overwhelming power of the duchy when the royal domains were confined to a narrow strip running from the Somme to the Loire, when the district south of that hardly acknowledged the king's supremacy at all, and when the Counts of Flanders and Anjou, and the Dukes of Burgundy, were scarcely less powerful than their suzerain himself. If the royal power were ever to increase, the Duke of Normandy must be humbled. So argued Henry, and forgetting in present necessity the benefits heaped upon his race by the Norman dukes, requited them by the most inveterate hostility. From this day the enmity of Normandy and France, lulled to sleep since the early days of William Longsword, began again, was transferred to England when Duke William added that kingdom to his dominions, and then, taking the form of national antagonism, lasted on with hardly a break till the end of the fifteenth century.

Bent thus upon humbling the dreaded power of Normandy, Henry is found supporting against the duke the rebellions which now and again break forth, and joining in the dangerous coalition which the jealousy of neighbouring princes raised against him , The movement extended from ducal Burgundy to the foot of the Pyrenees. The Count of Ponthieu, Theobald III. of Blois, even the Duke of Aquitaine and Count of Poictiers, who hitherto had rarely crossed the Loire, joined King Henry against the Bastard upstart.

This mighty host was divided into two detachments. One under Odo, King Henry's brother, was to attack Normandy from the north by way of Beauvais, and to advance on Rouen. The other, under the king himself, assembled at Mantes, and was to march on Lisieux and the sea. Thus surrounded by his foes, the Bastard might, they hoped, be utterly crushed or driven to the west. There, shorn of his eastern dominions, the flower of his ducal coronet, he might be suffered to retain the districts of the Bessin and the Cotentin, while the old grant of Charles the Simple should be restored to the successors of his throne, and Normandy, thus humbled, would no longer endanger the growing power of the king.

Their hopes were soon rudely to be overthrown by the strategy of Duke William. Advancing himself against the king, he held the royal forces in check as they crossed the border to the south. Meanwhile his forces, massed under his most trusty leaders, marched against Odo, surprised him in the town of Mortemer, and cut his contingent to pieces. A messenger despatched by the duke to the king rudely awakened him from his slumbers in the grey morning with the cry, 'Up, up. Frenchmen! ye sleep too long; go bury your friends that he dead at Mortemer!' A panic seized the royal forces, and Normandy was evacuated without a blow being struck against the duke himself.

Awed by William's superior strategy, which, hitherto he had had no opportunity of displaying, the coalition melted away, and William, after showing great leniency to his captive foes, enjoyed three years of peace, which he devoted to the government of his country and the reform of ecclesiastical abuses.

The peace of three years was soon over. A new coalition now arose against the duke, in which a new enemy appears—Geoffrey of Anjou.

The Counts of Anjou, one day to ascend the throne of England and gain the realm which Normandy had won, can be traced back to the ninth century, when Charles the Bald granted a dominion to Ingelger, a Breton woodman, first Count.

For a century, however, they bear no very important part in French affairs. Their district was a small one, marked out by no strong natural boundaries, and at the end of the tenth century they were entirely overshadowed by the power of their neighbours—the Counts of Blois and Champagne. With the accession of Fulk Nerra (the Black), their destinies began to rise. Under this powerful Count we first see that type of character displayed which henceforth so strongly marked his race. To the cool-headed and clear-sighted qualities of a consummate general he added a power of organization, a faculty of statesmanship, and an unscrupulousness in choice of means which soon raised Anjou into one of the most important powers in France, and which, coupled as they were with the most savage cruelty, made his name the terror of those days. His long reign is a series of triumphs. Brittany was defeated under Conan. Eudes of Blois was humbled at Pontlevoi. His dominions were extended to the south by the seizure of Saumur and the conquest of Touraine.

He had interfered in the affairs of France at the death of Robert, unsuccessfully supporting

Queen Constance and her second son Robert against King Henry. On his death he handed on Anjou—its borders extended, its powers consolidated—to his son Geoffrey Martel (the Hammer), a man hardly his inferior.

Continuing his father's policy, Geoffrey had wrested the city of Tours, the last city of Touraine which remained to them, from the house of Blois (1044) and this aggression had brought upon him the united forces of Normandy and France, then allies.

With the exception of this short quarrel, Normandy and Anjou had rarely come into contact. Their dominions nowhere touched each other: but between them lay the County of Maine, the possession of which they both desired, and which henceforth forms a constant source of dispute.

The claims of William to the County were founded upon the gift of Charles the Simple to Rollo. This claim, however, had been little more than nominal, and was now disputed by

Geoffrey as guardian of Hugh, the young Count of Maine.

This probably had been the motive of Geoffrey in supporting the rebels of Alençon in the early days of William (91), a quarrel which led to the occupation by William of the castle of Domfront on the soil of Maine, important as commanding the valley of the Mayenne, to the west of the Norman frontier, and that of Ambrières on the Varenne hard by. Since that time Geoffrey had in vain endeavoured to regain these castles, and now he eagerly embraced the opportunity of humbling his powerful rival, and joined the King of France. United by their hostility to the common foe, they concerted a joint invasion of the duchy. Entering the country from the County of Hiesmes, they advanced on Bayeux, ravaging as they went. Then turning to the south-east, they advanced on Caen, which was sacked. They now intended to cross the Dives, and harry the rich district of Lisieux to the east.

Meanwhile William, entrenching himself in his own castle of Falaise, had coolly waited his opportunity, determined to attack them as they returned gorged with spoil, their discipline relaxed by success.

The hour had now arrived. Rapidly marching from Falaise, he came upon them just as they were crossing the Dives. The king with the vanguard had already passed the stream and ascended the heights which overlook the Dives on the west bank. The rest were threading their way along a narrow causeway which led across low and marshy lands on the left bank. The tide was rising, and the ford would soon become impassable. This was the moment chosen by William for his attack, and the result was decisive. Huddled together on the narrow causeway, swept by the Norman arrows which we find here first mentioned, the main body of the army was annihilated, while Henry, prevented by the tide which now had risen from sending aid, looked on in helpless rage from the heights beyond at the ruin of his army.

This decisive victory, in which again the strategy of the duke had been pre-eminently displayed, ended the war. Peace was made, and two years afterwards both his enemies were removed by death.

Henry left his son Philip under the guardianship of the Count of Flanders his brother-in-law, father-in-law and trusty ally of William. Geoffrey's dominions were divided by his nephews Geoffrey and Fulk Rechin; Anjou and Saintonge falling to the former, to the latter the city and County of Tours. A short respite from war ensued of three years' duration. During that time we find William crushing out the remaining seeds of rebellion, banishing turbulent nobles and sternly repressing all who opposed his will. This is the date of the famous ordinance of the Curfew bell, issued at the synod of Caen. By this a bell was to be rung at evening when prayers should be offered, and all people should get themselves within and shut their doors. It was no doubt resorted to as a system of police, to secure the quiet of the country, and was subsequently introduced by William into England.

Normandy was then at rest; not so the busy duke. The County of Maine had, as we have seen, long been an object of desire, and now an opportunity offered to establish his authority there, and turn the vague grant to Rollo into possession.

We last left Maine in the hands of the young Count Hugh, under the guardianship of Geoffrey. Hugh died prematurely in 1051, and Geoffrey had occupied Le Mans, and driven out the widow and children of Hugh. But on the death of Geoffrey, Herbert, the son of Hugh, had appealed to William. He then commended himself to the duke, offered to hold Maine as a Norman fief, and giving his sister Margaret in betrothal William and to Robert, William's eldest son, promised him the succession if he himself should die childless. Two years afterwards Herbert died, and forthwith William claimed the fulfilment of the compact. The house of Anjou no longer disputed his title; but within the County the people refused to accept the Norman duke, and asserted the posed by rights of Walter of Mantes, the uncle, by marriage, of the late Count Herbert. His claim had no support but the wishes of the people. Three daughters, of whom Margaret was one, were still alive, and their title at least was better than that of Walter. Notwithstanding this, the dread of the Norman duke raised a formidable party, and war became inevitable if William did not mean to be baulked of his prey.

Neglecting the city of Le Mans, William ravaged the rest of the County, and by the terror which his cruelty inspired forced Walter to surrender the city and withdraw his claim. Thus, robbed of their leader, Maine submitted. Walter and his wife soon after died, some said poisoned by the duke, and Maine at last was added to the ducal coronet.

The conquest of Maine completes the history of William in Normandy. Important as that acquisition was in itself, it is more important as forming a prelude to the Conquest of England, on which our attention now centres.

CHAPTER XII.
THE CONQUEST OF ENGLAND.

On the death of Godwine, Harold had succeeded to his earldom of the West Saxons, and become the leading man in England. Godwine had been a man of ready speech and policy, but Harold was a man of action. With wider sympathies and knowledge than his father, he showed a more conciliatory spirit towards the remnant of the Norman party, while he maintained the true line of English policy. In the years that followed, the power of Harold steadily increased.

In 1055 Siward, Earl of Northumbria, died, and Northumbria was granted to Tostig, Harold's brother, whereby the influence of his house was temporarily extended to the north, while Gurth, and another brother, ruled in East Anglia. In the same year a dangerous competitor for the throne removed by death. Edward the Ætheling, the son of Edmund

Ironsides, had been recalled from Hungary by the Witan, the call being looked upon apparently as equivalent to a recognition of his claim to the succession. But hardly had he gained the shores of England when he died. His death, lamented by the English chroniclers as a national loss, is by calumny laid by them to the door of Harold, as that of the Ætheling Alfred had been attributed to Godwine. No doubt Harold was the chief gainer by his death. But this alone cannot be considered sufficient to establish his guilt, and Harold certainly was never accused of it during his life.

By the death of Edward the Ætheling, Harold's power was still further increased. Edgar the Ætheling and Margaret his sister now alone remained of the hereditary line. Of these one was a woman, and no instance had yet occurred of a queen sitting on the English throne. The other was too young to rule, and, if we may judge from his subsequent career, too weak to lead a party. From this date, therefore, Harold assumed a semi-royal position.

In 1062 we find him engaging in a Welsh war, and subduing the independent princes there, a campaign which added to the prestige of his name, and left him without dispute the greatest man in England.

Two years afterwards, according to the most probable account, Harold, driven by stress of weather on the coast of Ponthieu, was seized by its Count. No sooner did William hear of this than he demanded and obtained his release; and then, as the price of his assistance, extorted an oath from Harold, soon to be used against him. Harold, it is said, became his man, promised to marry William's daughter Adela, to place Dover at once in William's hands, and support his claim to the English throne on Edward's death. By a stratagem of William's, the oath was unwittingly taken on holy relics, hidden by the duke under the table on which Harold laid his hands to swear, whereby, according to the notions of those days, the oath was rendered more binding. Then, after aiding William to subdue Conan of Brittany, who had thrown off his allegiance to the duke, he returned to England.

Two years more, and Edward the Confessor died. Since the return of Godwine and the overthrow of the Norman party he had let things go as they would, and as death drew on he neglected more and more the affairs of state. Wrapt up in deeds of devotion, and in the foundation of his abbey of Westminster, he gave his kingdom hardly a thought, and passed away with an uncertain recommendation of Harold to the Witan, and with the gloomy prophecy on his lips which rang the death-knell of his race: 'Because those who are of most account in this kingdom—earls, bishops, abbots—are not what they seem to be, but are servants of the devil, God has given this land accursed of Him into the hand of the enemy within a year and a day.'

The Witan met. No mention was made of Edward's promise to William or of Harold's oath. Voices were raised for Edgar the Ætheling, even for Duke William; but the national feeling was too strong to elected accept the latter, and Edgar was as yet a stripling, and unfit to rule the kingdom at such a crisis. If the royal line was not to succeed, who better fitted for the post than the man whom Edward had recommended with his last breath, the man who for the last ten years had been king all but in name?

Harold was elected king. The families of Siward and Leofric did not oppose the choice, the opposition of Edwin and Morkar, grandsons of Leofric, who now held Northumbria, being perhaps bought off by the marriage of their sister Edith to Harold. Thus by 1066 the house of Godwine was seated on the English throne.

By this act the Witan reasserted their undoubted right to elect the king, and rejected at once the promise of Edward and the oath of Harold. No instance had yet occurred, indeed, of their thus electing a man not of princely birth; but in the case of Canute they had established their right to depart from the royal line, and in choosing Harold they best consulted England's interests, and chose the man in whom the best hope for the country lay. Hardly, however, was Harold on the throne than he was called to support his claim by arms.

His brother Tostig had been deprived of Northumbria for his cruelty and oppression, and banished the realm (1065). He now took the opportunity to avenge his wrongs, and with the sanction of William ravaged the coast of England. Then, forgetting his alliance with William, he turned to Harald Hardrada, king of Norway, with whom he agreed to divide the realm of England. Thus, then, this knight errant of the eleventh century, who had seen Constantinople, the Holy Land, and the southern shores of Italy, and who, once a landless wanderer, had now secured the kingdom of Norway, hoped to regain the crown of England once held by Canute. He came, the Saga tells us, bringing with him a mighty ingot—so large that twelve strong youths could scarcely bear it—part of the treasure collected in his southern expeditions, a treasure which was to pass as the reward of victory fir-^t to the

English Harold and then to William the Bastard.^

The invasion of Hardrada apparently had no connexion with that of William. It was carried out without his sanction, perhaps without his knowledge, and had it been successful, Hardrada would certainly have resisted the claims of the Norman duke. As it turned out, however, by calling off Harold's attention from the south at this moment, it materially contributed to William's ultimate success. The invasion was a formidable one. The isles of Shetland, Orkney, and Iceland, then owing nominal allegiance to Norway, sent their contingent, as well as the Danish settlers in Ireland. Even Malcolm of Scotland, who owed his crown to English help, influenced by his marriage with a princess of Orkney, lent his aid.

Hardrada, having first touched at the Orkneys and Shetlands to collect his forces, sailed south past the mouth of the Tyne, thence to Scarborough and to the Humber, ravaging as he went. Then, advancing up the Humber, he landed at Riccall, near York. In vain the Earls Edwin and Morkar attempted to defend their earldom; they were defeated, and even York opened its gates.

But the triumph of Hardrada was short-lived. Harold, hearing of the danger, at once marched north, and meeting his foes at Stamford Bridge, won a decisive victory. Tostig and Hardrada both fell, and the offer of Harold when treating before the battle, to give the King of Norway seven feet of earth or a little more, as he was taller than other men, was literally fulfilled. From the victorious battle-field of Stamford Bridge Harold was recalled by the news that William had already landed on the shores of Wessex to dispute his claim.

William was hunting in the forest of Rouen when he heard the news of Harold's election. He at once affected the most unfeigned astonishment, denounced Harold as a perjured man, and drawing up a specious claim, appealed to Christendom. In this appeal the wily diplomacy of William and his two chief friends, Lanfranc and William Fitz-Osbern, is strongly illustrated. He declared himself to be hereditary heir in his own right and that of his wife, and thus appealed to the idea of hereditary succession then growing in Europe. The religious feelings of the day were enlisted by his assumption of the position of an injured man punishing the false, perjured Harold. The Normans he reminded of the ill-feeling which had existed since his father's attempted invasion, and of the insults they had to avenge; the murder of the Ætheling Alfred when supported by Norman arms; the outrage inflicted on Eustace of Boulogne by the rude citizens of Dover; the subsequent deposition of a Norman archbishop, Robert of Jumieges, and the expulsion of the Normans by the proud, upstart family of Godwine. To the Pope, Alexander II., and his great minister Hildebrand, he speaks, probably at the suggestion of Lanfranc, of his invasion as a great missionary work which shall purify the corrupted Anglo-Saxon state and church, and bring England more closely under the sway of Rome. Thus, having united the suffrages of Europe, he rapidly gathered an army, and appealed to the ordeal of battle in vindication of his: claims.

While, then, we deny absolutely that William had any claim to the throne of England, we must at least acknowledge the skill by which he gathered up the threads, gave to his unjust claim the character of justice, and overcame the opposition of the Norman nobles, many of whom were unwilling to join in the enterprise. We cannot but admire the masterly statesmanship by which, in the face of an ever-watchful over-lord at Paris, he was enabled to gain the alliance, passive or active, of nearly all the powers of northern Europe, and prevented the Capetian king from allying himself with Harold or making a diversion by an attack on Normandy.

The army and transports were collected at the mouth of the Dives. Thence sailing to St.

Valery on the coast of Ponthieu, William waited until the south wind should blow, meanwhile spurring the religious enthusiasm of his army by frequent religious rites. At last the long wished-for wind arose, and, leaving Normandy to the care of his wife Matilda, he sailed for Pevensey.

The landing was effected without any opposition. Harold was still in the north, and had failed to keep an army together in the south. As William stepped upon the shore, he slipped and fell. The cry of the men, 'An evil omen this!' was answered by William's ready wit. 'By the splendour of God,' said William, holding up a handful of earth in his closed fist, 'I have taken seisin of my kingdom. The earth of England is in my hands.' Then ordering his ships to be beached and dismasted, that all idea of retreat might be prevented, he marched forwards to Hastings.

Meanwhile the forced marches of Harold had brought him to the south. Northumbria lent him no aid. The Earls Edwin and Morkar cared little for the fate of Harold or the south of England, and thought perhaps that the struggle might enable them to divide the kingdom and establish their own authority in the north. But the rest of England readily answered to his call, and with his army thus recruited, Harold marched to the hill of Senlac. This hill, of no great height, forms the last spur of the Sussex downs running from the west to the south-east. Connected with the higher ground behind by a narrow neck, it commands the broken ground at its foot, and stands in the face of an enemy approaching from the south.

The spot was well chosen, and here Harold, wisely deciding to await the Norman onslaught, formed a palisade in front of his position, just below the crest of the hill to the south. His army was composed entirely of footmen, but their weapons were of various kinds. Most had javelins and clubs, some only pitchforks, staves, and stones. These he marshalled to the right and left, while he himself, surrounded by his own 'house-carls' or body-guard, and the chosen warriors of Kent, Essex, and London, formed the centre round the golden dragon of Wessex and the royal standard. These were better protected with helmets, coats of mail, and shields. They wielded javelins and a double-handed axe, a formidable weapon which struck down horse and man at a blow. The strength of the English plainly lay in the closeness of their array and their defensive position. If the battle were to be won at all, this must be broken through, and, if possible, the English induced to leave their vantage ground.

William's quick eye at once discerned this, and he made his dispositions accordingly. His army was divided into three divisions. The Bretons, under Count Alan, on the left, the French and other mercenaries, under Roger of Montgomery, on the right. These were to attack the English on the flanks, while William, with his Norman troops, was to advance against the chosen men of Harold, and penetrate to the royal standard itself. These divisions each consisted of three different lines. First came the archers, slingers, and bowmen, thrown out in skirmishing order to harass the foe and disorder their close array; next the heavy-armed infantry who might support their attack, and by breaking through the palisades prepare the way for the mounted knights who formed the third line.

The preceding night had been passed in different ways by the two armies. The English eat, drank, and sang their national songs. The Normans prayed and confessed their sins. Two Norman prelates, Geoffrey of Coutances and Odo of Bayeux, William's half-brother, were with the army, and William, anxious to maintain the character of a leader in a religious war, stimulated his soldiers to vows and acts of devotion.

Thus morning arose upon the opposing hosts. Then William, reminding his soldiers that they came to punish the perjury of Harold and to wipe out the insults they had suffered, vowed to found an abbey on the battle-field if God should favour his cause, and ordered the attack. The archers led the way, and, discharging heavy flights of arrows, covered the advance of the heavy infantry. . This, however, failed to break through the palisades, and when the cavalry charged, they too were beaten back. Then with loud cries of 'Out, out!' the English attacked the Bretons on the left, who broke and fled.

The first charge had failed. William had fallen, it was said, and all seemed lost. At this crisis the bravery of William saved the day. While Odo rallied the fugitives, William tore his helmet from his head, crying, 'I live, and by God's grace I will conquer yet!' and once more led the attack. His horse fell, pierced by the javelin of Gurth, Harold's brother. He rose to his feet and felled his adversary with his mace, while Leofwine, another brother, was smitten by an unknown hand. Then seizing a stray horse, once more he led the cavalry on. In vain they threw themselves upon the serried ranks of the English, whose close array and greater weight told upon their foes, and the second attack was repulsed. The position was too strong to be gained by force. This William saw and had recourse to stratagem. Ordering a feigned retreat, he induced the English to leave their vantage ground and rush down with shouts of victory. Then William turned, and, charging the broken ranks unprotected by the palisades which they had left behind them, began to pierce the opposing masses. Still the English rallied. They formed a close array, and locking their shields together, stood their ground. Their wings were broken, and many an Englishman had died, but the centre still stood firm; still the standard waved where Harold fought.

One more device remained, and William seized upon it. The arrows could not pierce the English shields. He therefore gave the order to shoot up into the air. The effect was instantaneous. Helmets were pierced, eyes were put out, and the English, raising their shields to protect their heads, were overthrown by a renewed attack of infantry and cavalry.

As the sun went down, an arrow pierced Harold's eye. The Normans closed in upon the standard. The rest of English army broke and fled, and night found William victorious on the field of Senlac. In the morning the body of Harold was found where the standard stood, and, by the orders of William, obtained a decent burial. Thus ended the battle of Hastings, a battle between the old world and the new, of infantry armed with battle-axe, javelin, and pointed stake against the archers and the cavalry of the Normans. Two centuries at least were to pass before infantry learnt how to face the feudal array, and wiped out on the fields of Bannockburn and Courtrai the disgrace which Hastings cast upon their arms.

The battle of Hastings won, the next object of William was to secure the south-east, and especially Dover and Romney, the two most important of the Cinque Ports, commanding, as they did, the communication with the Continent. Thither, then, he directed his march, and not till he had received the submission of these places, as well as that of Canterbury and Winchester, the real capital of England, did he turn north to London.

The great want of the English after the death of Harold lay in the absence of a national leader. Had an Alfred or an Edmund Ironside arisen, William might yet have been driven from English soil; but in her greatest time of need no such man appeared. England might have looked to some member of the three great families—Godwine, Siward, Leofric—who had for so long shared the chief power in the land. Harold's brothers, however, had fallen with him on the field of Senlac. Of his sons no mention was ever made; no candidate from the house of Godwine, therefore, was forthcoming. Of the other two, Waltheof, the son of Siward, had not yet made himself a name, and although Edwin and Morkar, the grandsons of Leofric, would gladly enough have accepted the crown, their Mercian interests by no means tallied with those of Wessex. Once more men looked to the royal line, and the Ætheling Edgar, the grandson of Edmund Ironside, boy though he was, was chosen king. Such a leader did but weaken the national cause, and no sooner did William approach the city of London than all opposition faded away. The northern earls, Edwin and Morkar, would hazard nothing, and, dismayed by William's advance, made haste to retreat northwards. The bishops, after a brief display of resistance, counselled submission. The Witan sent in their adhesion to William, and at Christmas his coronation finally made him King of England.

Thus ended the national resistance of England. But the country was by no means conquered. East of a line from Norwich to Dorsetshire William was king. All north and west of that was yet to be won.

The national differences still surviving the Danish Conquest forbade the north to follow the lead of the south, and in the west the old spirit of independence which had so long struggled against Wessex, lasted on. As in the time of Alfred and of Edmund Ironside,

England had been conquered chiefly through her want of unity. Too little united to join against the common foe, she had allowed Harold to be defeated at Hastings; but her very want of unity led many to refuse the decision of a battle in which they had taken no share.

Under these circumstances the policy of William is somewhat difficult to justify. At Christmas he was William crowned. In the following March we find him leaving for Normandy, and relieving the anxiety of his wife Matilda whom he had left as regent. The apparent quiet of the country may have lulled him into a fancied security. The probable leaders of revolt, Edwin, Morkar, Waltheof, had submitted, and these he intended to take with him as hostages; possibly the step was taken with the intention of testing the fidelity of the English. Having therefore granted a charter to London, and appointed William Fitzosbern Earl of Herefordshire, and Odo Bishop of Bayeux, his half brother, regents, he left England for his duchy.

He was not long left in doubt. His own master-hand removed, the spirit of revolt revived. The government of the regents seems to have been needlessly harsh, and numerous local risings which only wanted unity of action to be really formidable, threatened the stability of his newly won throne.

The men of Kent united with Eustace of Boulogne, who was probably actuated by jealousy of William, and attacked the Cinque Ports. In the west, the English and Welsh united against the common foe under Edric the Wild and the prince of Wales, while Exeter, long looked upon as the dowry of the queens of England, rose at the instigation of Githa, the mother of Harold.

William, however, did not hurry back till the danger of foreign aid from Norway and Denmark warned him that he must strike at once. The country again was pacified, but no sooner did the expected help from Denmark come than revolt became once more general. The sons of Harold landed in Devonshire with a force from Ireland. In the north, the two Earls Edwin and Morkar, gaining the aid of Malcolm of Scotland, already the husband of Margaret sister of Edgar the Ætheling, threw off their allegiance, and the fire staff passed from village to village between Tees and Derwent. Waltheof held out at York. The Danes, joined by Edgar the Ætheling, ravaged the east coast, and Hereward, the last representative of southern resistance, occupied the Isle of Ely.

The danger was indeed great; but it served only to bring out more strongly the superiority of William as a tactician and a statesman, while, as he cast off all hopes of conciliation, his character becomes more stark and stern.

The real enemies to be disposed of were the Danes. These William bought off, and then turning upon the disorganised rebels, by a series of masterly marches he defeated them in detail. Three years it took him entirely to put down the rebellion; but by 1071 the last element of resistance was crushed out in the Isle of Ely, and England lay prostrate at his feet. Then crossing the Scottish border and the Lowlands, he penetrated to the heart of Scotland and forced Malcolm to swear allegiance.

The country had suffered terribly. For sixty miles between the Humber and the Tees it was reduced to a wilderness, and many English, despairing of success, left their native land, some to settle in the Lowlands, where they introduced English institutions, some to wander away to Constantinople, to give their services to the Emperors of the East in the bands of the Varangian Guards and defend the Eastern Empire from the attacks of the Normans of Apulia.

By 1071, then, William may be called the master of England. Edwin had fallen in a skirmish, Morkar, Waltheof, and Hereward had all submitted; there was no one to lead the English to revolt. The only part of England which remained unsubdued was the extreme west. This was not finally reduced till 1081, the date which also saw the final submission of the Welsh.

In tracing the course of William's Conquest of England, we are struck at every point with the different genius of the two peoples. We see the Saxons failing in their resistance, brave and sturdy though it was, through their strong spirit of localisation and consequent want of imperial unity, ever the secret of their weakness when called upon to resist their foes: the Normans excelling in their strong organization and administration executive and military, under their one great leader. While above all rise the stern features of William's character, with his unbending will and masterly qualities of generalship and strategy.

With the Conquest of England the Norman power reached its zenith. They had now succeeded to the fairest possession of their forefathers the Northmen. Scotland and Ireland were yet unwon, and on Spain they had lost their hold; but England and the northern shores of France were theirs, while in the south they had gained Calabria and were soon to be masters of Sicily.

The Norman name was now known to the whole of Europe. France, Germany, and Italy had long acknowledged their influence. Constantinople already dreaded their name, and was soon itself to be attacked in the Crusades by a mighty coalition led by them.

Of this great people William was now the most important figure. His countrymen in the south, though independent of him, were on friendly terms. In the north he held a kingdom larger than that of any of his neighbours, except perhaps the Emperor, while his suzerain, the King of France, he fairly outstripped in power.

Here then it will be well to pause and consider the character of the Conquest, and of William's policy to his newly acquired country.

CHAPTER XIII.
WILLIAM'S POLICY TOWARDS THE CONQUERED COUNTRY.

There were three classes in the country with whom William had to deal, and these for convenience sake we will take in order.

To understand the policy of the Conqueror towards the English, it is necessary to take a retrospect of their constitutional history. Anglo-Saxon society, by the time the English Conquest was completed, consisted of four ranks. The eorl, or noble by birth; the ceorl, or free by birth; English læt, and the theow or slave. Of these the two former only were considered full free. The læt was really an inferior ceorl, enjoying personal freedom, but holding his land of some lord upon whom he was dependent. The theow or slave, a small unimportant class, consisted of those who had lost their liberty for debt or other causes. The two latter classes were probably, in the West of

England at least, largely recruited from the conquered Kelts. The tribes thus constituted were commanded by leaders who appear under different names. Of these the ealdorman was the chief magistrate in times of peace, the heretoga the leader in war. In time these two offices were combined in one person under the name of cyning or king.

The mark system, or custom of holding lands in common, had nearly if not entirely passed away, and each freeman had a right to a certain portion of land granted out to him after the conquest of the country, and called his 'allodial property.' This property, the possession of which was a necessary condition of full tribal membership, he held in full ownership without any rent or service, except those included in the term 'trinoda necessitas,' the requirements of which were to serve in the national militia, repair roads and bridges, and keep up the defences of the country.

What remained after this allotment was called the folk-land, and this could not be granted out to any without the consent of the whole tribe given in its 'gemot' or assembly. If so granted, it was termed 'boc-land,' or land booked out, and in that case the terms of tenure varied.

The people settling down on these terms formed themselves into political self-governing societies. Of these the unit was the *township*, a rural division of varying limits surrounded by the tun, or quickset hedge. A cluster of townships formed the hundred, and a cluster of hundreds the shire. Each of these had their separate courts.

In the court of the township all the freemen of the township had a right to sit, and there their elected representative, the town reeve, settled their petty disputes, collected their contributions to the revenue, and summoned the militia when necessary.

In the court of the hundred the several townships of which the hundred was formed were represented by their parish priest, their reeve, the lords of lands, and four elected men.

Its presiding magistrate was the hundredman, elected in the Hundred court. But the judges were at first the whole body of the suitors, and subsequently a representative body of twelve men capable of declaring the law, who for convenience sake were entrusted with the judicial business of the hundred. Here more important disputes were settled. Theoretically every suit began here, and an appeal lay to the. Shire court. The hundred-man led the hundred to the militia, and the hundred formed the basis of assessment for taxation.

The shire was probably originally the sub-kingdom, and the shire court the court or 'gemot' of that sub-kingdom. But as the separate kingdoms became united, the shire became a division of the kingdom, a collection of hundreds, and the Shire court the highest and most important of the local courts. Its suitors were the same as those of the Hundred courts which fell within the shire. Its officers were the ealdorman, the sheriff (shire-reeve), and the bishop. Of these, the ealdorman represented the old sub-king, who, as the sub-kingdoms were gradually united, became a national officer. He was appointed by the king and Witenagemot, and had the command of the whole militia of the shire. The sheriff in practice was always nominated by the king, and was his judicial and fiscal officer, collecting the royal revenues and presiding in the court. The bishop, sitting with the other two, decided questions of ecclesiastical law. The judges, as was universally the case in these local courts, were not the officers, but all the suitors to the court—that is, all who had a right to sit there. Here, however, as in the Hundred court, the office of judges was subsequently limited to certain representative men, often twelve in number.

The ecclesiastical divisions of the country nearly resembled the political. The parish was identical with the township, the bishoprick with the shire; and the ecclesiastical and political organization borrowed much from one another.

It was in the Shire court that all important cases, civil and criminal, were decided. An appeal lay from the inferior courts to this court, while from the Shire court the appeal lay to the king in the Witenagemot. In civil matters it settled disputes and witnessed transfers of land. But the most important part of its jurisdiction was the criminal.

Let us then suppose the offender caught, and follow him to his trial. His judges, observe, are the freemen of the district, assembled in their own 'folk-moot,' or later, the twelve representative men. The ealdorman, sheriff, and bishop are only officers of the court; they preside over it, and the sheriff sees the law executed, but they do not judge the accused. Here then, in the very origin of our history, we have the right of every Englishman to be tried by his peers.

Now the accused might be presented for trial by the judgment of the Hundred court. In that case he was looked upon as one convicted by common opinion, and was judged accordingly.

He might indeed appeal to the 'ordeal,' a form of trial in which the accused, appealing to the judgment of God, walked across red-hot bars of iron or was thrown into water. But even here, if he escaped unhurt, he was still considered a bad character, and though relieved from greater punishment had to fly the realm.

But next, he might be accused by a private individual. In that case he was allowed to bring witnesses called 'compurgators,' people who swore to the truth of his oath and thus attested the respectable character of the accused, and purged him from the imputations cast upon him. Now, if the accused could bring enough of those compurgators to balance the evidence of the other side, he would be acquitted, and, in considering the question, the popular judges estimated the weight of each compurgator by his rank. Thus an eorl's word would be as valuable as that of six ceorls, and an earldorman's evidence might outweigh that of a whole township.

No doubt this was a rough and ready way of administering justice, and there may have been a temptation to get rid by this means of an unpopular man; but, at least, the question of guilt or innocence was left to those who were most likely to know the probabilities of the case from a man's antecedents.

Finally, if a man could not bring sufficient compurgation, he might go to the ordeal, and if he passed that safely would be considered acquitted by the direct interposition of God.

Punishment generally took the form of pecuniary fines, that of death being unknown except in cases of treason, sacrilege, witchcraft, and theft where the thief was caught in the act. Injury to life and limb was compounded for by the wer-gild, paid to the injured man, or to his family in case of death, and the wiht-geld, or fine to the state. The wer-gild of each man was arranged on a sliding scale according to his rank—that of an eorl being greater than that of a ceorl, and so on.

The system of police bore the same local character which we have seen so strongly developed in the Anglo-Saxon institutions. It was based upon the idea of mutual responsibility. For this purpose the hundreds were divided into tithings, and by a law of Canute's everyone was bound to belong to a tithing, while by the laws of Edgar every landless man was forced to have a lord to answer for him in the courts, and every man a surety to answer for him if he were absent when required.

Such was the local and judicial organization of the Anglo-Saxon institutions in their earliest form. But before the Norman Conquest several modifications had occurred. These will best be summed up under the heads—(1) Growth of thaneship; (2) Rise of territorial jurisdiction; (3) Growth of towns or burghs.

(1) *Growth of Thaneship.*—Side by side with the democratic constitution of all German tribes, there had existed a peculiar institution known as the Comitatus. Each ealdorman or

king was allowed to collect around him a body of personal followers called his gesiths, or his thanes; representing a condition of things not unlike that described in the Homeric poems, where each chief has a following of personal attendants called his ἑταῖροι or companions. These warriors were bound to their lord by the closest ties of personal dependence, and after the conquest received grants, either from the undivided 'folk-land 'which remained over after the freemen had received their share, or on the domains of the ealdorman or king. These thanes might be ceorls or eorls themselves, holding lands of their own, or might have no freehold of their own; in either case they were at first looked upon as an inferior class by the independent eorls and ceorls. But in time, as the power of the king increased, they began to borrow dignity from his advance. In times of war such nobles by service, forming chiefly a military class, became the natural leaders. Their privileges too were increased by the royal grants. From them the king chose his officers, his ealdormen, sheriffs, and even bishops; and thus a class of nobility by service arose, which in the end superseded entirely the nobility by birth.

The custom once begun, eorls and ceorls pressed into the service of the king. The ealdorman, now falling back into a national officer, surrounded himself with thanes, and the bishop's and king's thanes followed suit. Then the eorls and ceorls, abandoning their independence, which day by day became more precarious, made haste to commend themselves to some lord, and in return for the commendation received the benefit of security.

Meanwhile, a property qualification became an essential requirement for the position of a thane, who thus assumed a territorial rather than a personal character.

Finally, under Athelstan the principle of lordship became compulsory. Everyone was bound to attach himself to some lord, and the lordless man was looked upon as an outlaw.

Under these influences the classes of eorl and ceorl entirely passed away. The class of eorls merged in that of thane, a term which now became equivalent to noble or gentle, while the ceorls either became thanes or were degraded into a semi-servile class.

Thus thaneship, at the time of the Norman Conquest, had become the central institution of the state, and the twofold rank of eorl and ceorl was lost in that of thane.

(2) *Rise of Territorial Jurisdiction.*—At the first settlement of the English, the greater lords had enjoyed in some cases independent jurisdiction. That is to say, where a township lay on their property, although the constitution was the same as in the free township, the reeve was appointed by them, and they enjoyed the privileges and undertook the duties which elsewhere belonged to the free^ holders. Such townships virtually formed manors, though the name itself is of Norman origin; and as the principle of thaneship grew, these jurisdictions increased, partly by royal grants, partly by

commendation of whole townships to a neighbouring thane. Gradually by the grant of 'sac' (jurisdiction in matters of dispute), and 'soc' (the right of holding courts for their personal and territorial dependants), the thanes gained exemption from the jurisdiction of the Hundred court, though still subject to that of the Shire, and the payments formerly due to the Hundred court were now made to the thane. Thus their territorial jurisdiction rapidly increased, and the idea of possession of land and jurisdiction went hand in hand; these private jurisdictions encroaching largely upon the popular courts.

Meanwhile the jurisdiction of the king increased. From being merely the hearer of appeals in the Witenagemot he began to be looked upon, as the origin of all justice. The number of pleas reserved to the crown ('crown pleas') increased, and these were judged by the royal officers in the local courts.

Lastly, about the time of Canute, the king in some cases delegated his powers to some great land-owner, who thus became the superior judicial officer in his district, superintended the popular courts, and usurped their rights.

From all these causes the lower popular courts of township and hundred decreased in influence, while the manorial courts became more and more important, and threatened, at the time of the Norman Conquest, soon to supersede them entirely.

(3) *Growth of Burghs.*—The growth of burghs tended to the same end. Originally the Anglo-Saxons were not fond of municipal life, and neglected any remains of Roman organisation which may have survived among the British after the Roman occupation, the township, it must be remembered, being in no sense a town as we should call it, but a rural subdivision of the free community. But in time the villages grew; the smaller 'burhs' became a kind of civic township, with their borough-moot corresponding to the rural township court; the larger, comprising a collection of townships, each with their separate borough-moot, gained

an organization similar to that of the hundred, with their Ward-mote or civic Hundred court.

These larger towns, standing apart from the neighbouring hundred, would enjoy certain rights of jurisdiction independent of the Hundred but subject to the Shire court, and in some cases paid a composition by which they gained immunity from arbitrary exactions.

By the time of the Conquest, therefore, there existed the court of the township, manorial courts, and the borough courts; above these the Hundred court, from the jurisdiction of which the two latter had, perhaps, to some extent emancipated themselves; and above all, the Shire court, to which they all were subject and to which the appeal lay.

The local government stopped at the Shire court, the central was entrusted to the Witenagemot. The institution of this assembly is probably due to a somewhat later date, after the kingdom had been consolidated and the power of the king established. It was therefore the creation of royalty, and not a representative assembly. On great occasions, indeed, the Witenagemot was attended by a concourse of people, to whom its decision was announced, and who, by their applause, were supposed to give the national assent. But none had any right to sit, or enjoyed any deliberative vote, except the counsellors of the king, the bishops, the ealdormen, and some of the greater or king's thanes.

The powers assumed by this body were, in theory at least, very extensive. It was the supreme legislative and deliberative assembly of the kingdom, and the court of final appeal in judicial matters. With the king it could do anything, and without it nothing of importance could be done. The king, with its counsel and consent, passed laws ecclesiastical as well as civil, levied taxes, made grants out of the folkland, deliberated on peace or war, elected bishops and ealdormen, and carried on the whole machinery of government. It even claimed and exercised the right of electing and deposing the king, though the election was by custom confined to the royal family, with a presumption in favour of the representative of the eldest branch, if of fit age and character to govern, and, in later times at least, the nomination of the dying king was held to have considerable weight. Still, in the exceptional cases of Canute and his sons Harold Harefoot and Harthacnut, and of Harold, the Witan even departed from the royal line.

The constitutional fabric was crowned by the king himself. From the position of mere leader of his tribe in peace and war, the representative of his people, he had, by the gradual consolidation of the kingdoms into one, gained a constitutional and territorial position. He was no longer king of the West Saxons, but king of England. He enjoyed considerable revenues, and had a large private demesne, which in those days, when the expenses of government were small owing to the development of local organisation, made him almost entirely independent of the Witan for money.

He was the supreme executive officer of the realm, and all paid him personal allegiance, while in his circuits he superseded by his presence the powers of all the local courts. Moreover, as we draw near the Norman Conquest, we find his powers steadily increasing. The Witan daily became a narrower body, more and more the mere officers of royalty, before which their powers faded.

The 'folk-land' was now considered as the king's royal demesne, and practically he disposed of it as he would. The growth of thaneship added to his personal influence. His jurisdiction grew by the multiplication of pleas of the crown and by the extension of the idea that all offences were violations of his (the king's) peace, and with the development of the territorial idea he gradually became the lord of his people and their land.

The question now arises, Did feudalism exist in England before the Norman Conquest? From this sketch it will be seen that many of its germs at least were there. The *personal tie* was to be found in the relation of lord to thane, and the thane paid service to his lord, especially his 'heriot,' or gift of the best horse or suit of armour on his death. Even land was sometimes held on the terms of military service.

The possession of land had become a necessary qualification for nobility and freedom. Territorial jurisdiction had in many cases arisen, and the manorial courts were very similar to those of the feudal system, while the king had become the lord of the land of the nation.

But Continental feudalism had not as yet arisen. Continental feudalism has been defined as 'a complete organization of society through the medium of land-tenure, in which from the king to the landowner all are bound together by obligation of service and defence.' Government and jurisdiction were based upon this system, and whilst the lord exercised jurisdiction over his tenants he was considered the lord of the land which they held of him.

Hence the main distinction between that system and the Anglo-Saxon lay in these points, (1) Although when Canute divided England into four great earldoms he introduced a system very similar to feudal government, feudal government proper never existed. The official magistrates had not become entirely hereditary. The ealdorman did not enjoy fiscal, legislative, and judicial independence as the feudal nobles did abroad. The local courts of the shire, hundred, and township still existed, and the former were supreme even over manorial courts within the shire. Nor was the central government organized on feudal principles, nor the Witenagemot in any sense a feudal court. (2) Although the *personal* tie was there, the *real* one was not; that is, the land had not become the tie or bond between the king and his people or between lord and thane. Though all were obliged to have some lord, they could choose their lord, and if they held lands of him this did not form the tie between them, but the personal commendation; and many held no land of their lord, but possessed lands of their own. Lastly, many landowners enjoyed territorial jurisdiction, but it extended over men whose lands were in no sense held of them.

But if feudalism did not exist, it was on the point of arising, and but for the Norman Conquest would probably have been developed as it was abroad.

Such were the institutions of the people over whom William had been elected king. William, it must be remembered, did not claim his tide to the throne by conquest. The attitude assumed by him was that of the lawful claimant to the throne, who, finding himself unjustly ousted by the perjured usurper Harold, had appealed to the judgment of God on the battlefield of Hastings, and there asserted the rightfulness of his cause. It was under this pretext that he had gained the moral support of Europe and the blessing of the Pope, and after the battle he had referred the matter to the Witan, who had freely elected him as king. On this election primarily he based his right. He styled himself the successor of Edward the Confessor, and the name of Harold was omitted, as that of a usurper.

He had, therefore, neither the opportunity nor the inclination entirely to overthrow the nationality of the country or to destroy its time-honoured institutions, but in theory became as truly a national king as Canute. It was in this spirit that he devoted himself to the task which lay before him of adapting the institutions of his newly-won country to those which he brought from Normandy, and to the altered circumstances of the times. And it is in this work that the political genius of William and his truly Norman powers of adaptation are forcibly illustrated.

From the preceding sketch the weakness and strength of the Anglo-Saxon institutions will be understood. Their strength lay clearly in their local and social aspect; in the development of the lower grades of constitutional life; in the healthy local self-government found in the organisation of the shire, the hundred, the township, and the borough; in the popular character of their justice; and in their self-dependence, their quiet and peace-loving character.

In all this they were strong; but in the higher ranges of constitutional life they failed. The connexion between the local self-governing communities and the central government was feeble. The administrative machinery by which the king might maintain the superintendence and carry on the central government was inadequate and ill-arranged. The relation between the local courts of justice and that of the king, who held a general superintendence over them, and to whom lay the ultimate appeal, was ill-defined.

This William clearly saw, and he acted accordingly. The local courts were preserved intact, and the English language was allowed there. The number of manorial courts was increased by royal grant, but no other change was made. No difference was made in the local administration of justice except that the trial by combat was added to the compurgation and ordeal for the use of Normans. The privileges of towns were left untouched, and those of London confirmed by royal charter.

The system of mutual responsibility was extended in the system of frankpledge, by which the police arrangements were carried out by sections of ten men, mutually responsible for each other.

The militia system was continued, and the 'trinoda necessitas' maintained.

So far, William acted as an English king and perpetuated national institutions. But in the relations between the central government and the king many modifications were introduced. The Witenagemot was continued indeed, but turned into a feudal court, the 'Commune Concilium' of the Norman kings, in which the members sat as feudal lords. A sort of committee of this, the 'Curia Regis,' was established, which, besides its character as a council of deliberation and legislation, formed the court of ultimate appeal, in some cases a court of first instance, and kept the local courts in order. Of this court the presiding officer was the Justiciary, an officer of purely foreign origin. For the full development of his powers we must wait till the reign of Henry I., but under William he was generally the regent of the kingdom in the king's absence, and probably soon began to assume his later position of supreme judicial and financial officer of the realm.

The government of the shires was entrusted to earls, the successors of the old ealdormen. But William avoided the fault of Canute. He did not carve out England into great earldoms; he confined his earldoms to one shire, and was careful, with a few exceptions to be mentioned hereafter, to keep the earls in due subordination to himself, and to render them more entirely an official class.

The sheriffs, too, were made more dependent on the king, and became his representatives in all fiscal matters, thus binding the local courts and local organization to the central government, and preventing undue independence from arising. These reforms did not, indeed, arrive at their perfect form till the reign of Henry I. and Henry II., nor had William, a man of war, troubled as he was by continual disturbances, time fully to complete his schemes. But he introduced the germ of the future Anglo-Norman government; and by preserving what was strongest in the Anglo-Saxon system, and strengthening what was weak by new elements, by his stern will he welded the two into a compact whole, with all the elements of stability. And to this day these two elements lie side by side, each betraying their origin and attesting the political wisdom of William: the local organization emanating from the English people, the administrative and financial system centred round the Norman king.

To the lowest classes, indeed, the Norman Conquest was a boon. The Normans, unaccustomed to actual slavery, confused the lower classes in the common class of 'villeins' or 'servi.' The latter probably represented the Anglo-Saxon 'theows' and the landless 'ceorls,' and seem to have held the position of landless labourers. The former were chiefly formed of those 'ceorls' who before the Conquest had failed to rise to the rank of thanes, and had fallen into a semi-servile class. The position of the 'villeins' seems to have been far better now than it became later. If they might not leave the land without the lord's consent, they were at least safe in the possession of their homes. They had to till the soil of his demesne, but had a remedy against the violence of their master. The servus and villein alike might be manumitted by the Church, and at a later date, if they could escape to a town and live there as members of a guild for a year and a day, they were held to have earned their freedom. But to the higher and middle classes it was different. Although the Anglo-Saxons were still allowed to enjoy their time-honoured institutions and customs, and the policy of William was conciliatory, their condition was not a happy one. Their laws and language, indeed, were not swept away by any formal legislative enactments, but in the hands of Norman officers the spirit of legal administration was changed, the English ceased to be the court language, and the country was, as we shall see, gradually feudalised. The Chronicles do not complain of suppressed nationality, but are full of the legal and fiscal oppression: 'The king was so stark, and took of his subjects many marks of gold and more of silver.'

William, after the first submission of England, affected, and probably intended, to rule mildly and mercifully. But the constant rebellions which subsequently broke out brought out the sternness and indifference to suffering which stain his character. The whole country between Tees and Humber was reduced to a perfect waste, and for nine years was entirely untilled. The depopulation which went on is clearly seen from the records of Domesday Book. Thus, Oxford, in the Confessor's time, had 721 houses; in William's only 243. York under the former contained 1,607; under the latter only 967.

The confiscations, at first confined to those who had actually fought at Hastings, rapidly increased, and at the end of the reign there were no Anglo-Saxon earls, only one Anglo-Saxon bishop, and a few abbots and great landowners remaining. The people saw their wealth and offices transferred to Norman barons, and groaned under their cruelty and oppression. Their country became only a part, and that not the most important part, of al Norman kingdom, and her interests were continually sacrificed to those of Normandy. Her king was more often abroad than in England, while in his absence the Normans ground down the people. In every way they suffered much, yet it was the happiest thing for England in the end. When we remember the want of combined action and political unity which marked the preceding, history of England, when we remember the power of the two great families of Leofric and Siward, and the independence of Northumbria and the jealousy with which Edwin and Morkar looked upon the ascendency of Harold, we must allow that had he succeeded quietly and transmitted his crown to his successors, he would have enjoyed only a partial supremacy over a large part of the country. His position was not unlike that of Hugh Capet, first king of France, and probably, as in France, the earls would long have maintained their independence. Continental feudalism, too, all the elements of which we have seen existed in England, would probably have arisen with its anarchy, isolation, and class privileges, and the condition of England might soon have resembled that of France. Far better for her was it that she should be conquered and reduced to submission and unity, even by the cruel hands of the Norman kings. Far better was it that she should suffer a temporary overthrow of her national being. For thus she gained what was wanting in her own political condition; the growth of feudalism was checked, and after a century or so of compression and pruning which, though severe, was necessary for future growth, all that was valuable in the Anglo-Saxon institutions reasserted itself and became the primary basis of our later constitution. We should remember, too, that by the Conquest England was brought into far closer contact with the Continent, and this, too, at an important epoch. This was clearly for the good of England. The Anglo-Saxon, as is well illustrated by the character of his historical literature, had no European sympathies, hardly any English imperial ones. His interest, his sympathies were entirely local. He had no sense of a common brotherhood of men, a commonwealth of nations. He set little value on things removed from his own personal observation, and his ideas were thus essentially narrow and confined. By the Norman Conquest all this was changed. England, becoming as she did part of an Anglo-Norman kingdom, was forced to embrace wider sympathies, began to feel herself really a member of Europe, and thus lost that narrowness and exclusiveness which so clearly marks her earlier history.

Lastly, the Anglo-Saxon character, institutions, and social life seem to have required some new infusion of blood, and this the Normans gave. The Anglo-Saxon character seems to have had all the characteristics of stability, but not of advance; of solidity, but not of sprightliness. It required the Norman element, deeply influenced as it was by the French character, to give the necessary life and vigour, and without the Normans, as it has been well said, 'England would have been mechanical, not artistic; brave, not chivalrous; the home of learning, not of thought.' In no long time the two peoples began to amalgamate, and a healthy, strong, and vigorous people was the result, uniting the strength of the Norman and Anglo-Saxon characters, which soon began to multiply more rapidly than other European nations, and which now has spread to every part of the inhabited globe.

In spite, then, of the temporary misery which England must have undergone, although we naturally lament over the fall of Harold, the king of the Anglo-Saxons, as a national loss, and over Hastings as a national defeat, we can but acknowledge that the Norman Conquest was a necessary and beneficial experience in our history, from which, as far as we can see, the greatest benefits have flowed.

The advantages which England gained by the Norman Conquest will further appear from a review of the policy of William towards the Norman nobles.

The Norman nobles had been induced to aid William in his invasion by promises of wealth and power, and these promises had now to be fulfilled. They had no reason to complain. The confiscated estates of the conquered were largely conferred upon them, and their manors were granted to them with exemption from the jurisdiction of the Hundred court. They practically monopolised all the important offices of state. They also enjoyed the position of counsellors of the king. So far William satisfied their claims. But they had been accustomed to a feudal form of government, with its anarchy and independence, and many of them longed, no doubt, to become great feudal lords in England.

Thus William was brought face to face with the question: how far should he introduce Continental feudalism into England?

In examining his policy in this respect, it will be well to consider feudalism again under its twofold divisions—(1) a system of land-tenure, (2) a system of government.

To the feudal system of land-tenure William had been long accustomed, and to it there was no objection. Consequently, all the lands which were confiscated from the Anglo-Saxons were granted out to his Normans on feudal terms, and became 'feudal manors,' and the 'folk-land' was turned absolutely into crown property. The Anglo-Saxon landowners still held their lands by their old tenure; but owing to the repeated revolts, few of these remained at the end of

William's reign, and those few, following the now almost universal custom, either made terms with the king himself or with some neighbouring lord, and consented to hold their lands as feudal vassals.

Thus, by a gradual process, the feudal tenure of land became universal in England, and was worked up into a system by the Norman lawyers.

But with the government of the country the case was different. William had seen the evil results of the Continental system, the anarchy, the isolation, the weakening of the royal authority which it produced, and was determined to prevent this in England. Accordingly, in his grants to his Norman nobles he refused to carve out principalities for his followers. He gave them manors scattered over England; and, while allowing them the right of jurisdiction in their manors, he strictly limited their powers, in most cases by the appeal to the Hundred court, in all by direct appeal to himself, and kept them in due subordination by his royal processes or circuits. The earls were only set over single shires, and the growth of independence thereby checked. The great lords were allowed no independent rights of coining, nor of making laws; all these matters being reserved to the king himself. Exceptions indeed were made. The four Counties Palatine— Chester, under Hugh Lupus; Shrewsbury, under Roger Montgomery; Durham, and Kent, were erected, in which the governors enjoyed rights very similar to those of the feudal barons abroad. Of these the earldom of Chester was the most important, and may be taken as type of the rest, though it enjoyed greater rights than any other. The Earl of Chester was lord of all the land in the shire except that in the hands of the bishop. He had a council of the barons in the Palatinate, his own judicial courts, his own staff of judges, constable, steward, and other officers. Offences were said to be done against *his* peace and not that of the king, and all acts were in his name. In fact, he was feudal sovereign of Cheshire, as the King of

England was in Normandy. So entirely did the Palatine jurisdictions stand apart from the rest of England, that those of Chester and Durham, the only two which survived the Conqueror's reign, were not represented in the national Parliament till the reigns of Henry VIII. and Charles II. respectively, while that of Durham retained its independent courts till 1836.

These Counties Palatine were so granted because they formed the outposts against danger from without: Shrewsbury and Chester against the Welsh; Durham against the Scots; and Kent against invasion from the Continent. Here great centralisation and authority were required against surprise. But even here the political foresight of the Conqueror did not forsake him. Two of these, Durham and Kent, were granted to ecclesiastics, whereby they were prevented from becoming hereditary, and that of Kent was not revived after the fall of Odo of Bayeux.

Lastly, in 1086, taking advantage of a threatened invasion from Norway, William made every landowner in England take an oath of homage to him *immediately*, instead of demanding it only of his 'tenants-in-chief,' who, in their turn, might exact it from their own tenants. By this act he destroyed the essence of feudal government, which consisted in the gradation of ranks one beneath the other, the lowest holding of that immediately above and responsible to that alone; the 'tenants-in-chief,' or those who held of the king himself, being alone responsible to him.

Thus, while elsewhere a vassal was bound to follow his immediate lord even when rebelling against the king, and could not be punished for so doing, in England everyone who took arms against the king was held guilty of treason.

In this policy William was largely aided by the insular position of England, and by the comparatively small extent of the kingdom. By the former, the factious nobles were prevented from speedily gaining assistance against their king as they did abroad. By the latter, centralisation of government was rendered easy, and the centrifugal tendencies of the times checked.

Thus, in the government of England, the balance of power lay clearly on the side of the king; while in France this was destroyed in favour of the baronage. But the French view was taken by the Norman barons; and after William had crushed out the local resistance of the Saxons, he had to meet with the rebellions of his feudal vassals in Normandy and England.

The results of the policy of William are among the most important facts of early English history, and we may fairly say that it is to William in no little degree that we are indebted for our later constitutional government. Not that he in any way anticipated, or could have anticipated it, nor that, had he done so, he would have welcomed the prospect, but he was in this matter what most men are after all, the servants of a Master they cannot resist. It would seem that every nation in the course of its development must pass through a stage, a period of absolutism, more or less declared. Such a schooling is necessary to break down the independence and privileges of the nobility, to fuse races and classes together, and to give them common interests and common sympathies for which they in turn may struggle against the sovereign's will. This schooling England underwent under the stern rule of her Anglo-Norman kings; while France, sacrificed as she was to the anarchy of feudalism, put off her schooling till late, when it became doubly oppressive, in fact, a tyranny.

Again, society must first develope a strong, healthy, legal system before she can advance to anything like real and practical freedom. Without such a system to rally round, liberty becomes anarchy, equality a contradiction in terms, since equality before the law is the only one that can exist, and without law equality is sacrificed to the might of the strongest. This, again, the strong rule of the Anglo-Norman kings gave to England, whereas in France it did not grow up till late, then only to add still further links to the chain of absolute and irresponsible despotism.

Let us, keeping these two points in view, try and trace the different results of feudalism in England and France. France the independence of the feudatories from the crown was practically all but complete. The nation resembled in fact rather a confederacy of independent princes than a united nation under one king. These feudal princes enjoyed all or nearly all royal rights, and, proud of their independence, affected to despise their weak over-lord at Paris. Trusting to their own great power, they refused to unite, except in a fitful way, with one another, and caring nothing for the classes below them, divided their lands among a host of inferior barons who might assist them against their king, and who joined with them in grinding down the lower classes. Hence arose isolation in every form. Isolation of one part of France from the other, which checked the growth of national unity. Isolation amongst the nobles, which eventually contributed to their fall. Isolation between classes, military and non-military, which prevented any union. Law, too, never for years attained to the position of any real system. One half of France was called 'le pays du droit coutumier,' clearly showing the absence of any definite system, and in the rest of France, 'le pays du droit écrit,' the law was continually being evaded, altered, and destroyed by the anarchy which existed. Hence in France we see an utter absence of cohesion, an utter want of community of interests between all classes and all parts of the country. On this and out of this rose the power of the crown. Itself the only organised power, it slowly but surely broke in upon the anarchy. The independent feudatories, prevented by their jealousy from uniting against the common foe, were either subdued or absorbed in detail. The people, seeking in the growth of the kingly power a defence from their hated over-lords, joined the king, and while they contributed materially to the consolidation of his power, omitted, in their hot haste, to secure themselves against future extravagances of prerogative. When then under Louis XIV. the crown had absorbed all the independent principalities, and the political influence of the nobles was gone, nothing remained to stay its despotism except the social privileges of the nobles, which rendered them hated while they were not feared, and led to their eventual overthrow.

From this England was saved by the wise policy of William. The nobles, deprived of their independence at the time of the Conquest, struggled hard against their masters, rebelled continually, though without success, under William I., Rufus, and Henry I., who were thus forced in some measure to unite with the nation against them. Overthrowing the central authority, they triumphed for a short time under Stephen, but, absolutely, defeated under Henry II., were obliged to change their tactics. They now sought alliance with the classes below them, made common cause with them, and at their head marched forth, under John and Henry III., to wrest constitutional and national privileges from an overgrown prerogative, and to lay the basis of a free and limited government in which the interests of the whole nation were considered. Hence in England no great gulf existed between classes, between the military or noble and the non-military or ignoble. There was no difference in the eyes of the law between noble and commoner. A few privileges the nobles had, but none in anyway onerous to the rest of the community, such as exemption from taxes, as in France. They had to seek for this power by showing themselves worthy leaders of a great constitutional cause, by becoming the leading statesmen of the day, and winning the respect if not always the love of the classes below them, who for a long time looked to them as their natural leaders against the king. While thus England was ruled by an aristocracy, it was an aristocracy which claimed no irksome privileges, and which in some measure represented the interests of the nation.

Again, of all aristocracies ours is the least exclusive and the most democratic. It is constantly receiving new members from the commonalty, whilst its younger branches are continually sinking into the ranks of the commonalty. Abroad all the sons of a noble belong to the nobility; in England only the eldest son succeeds to the political privileges of his father, and the rest, with some slight social privileges, are counted as members of the commons. Thus the nobility and commonalty are welded together, and there is no broad line of division between the two, as is the case abroad.

The whole nation, presenting a common resistance to arbitrary power, gradually encroached upon the irresponsible prerogative of its kings, and vindicated for itself national privileges; and England having early passed her schooling days, started forth into vigorous manhood, receiving one valuable legacy at least from the hand of her stern schoolmaster, a thoroughly organised and fully developed system of law, which might form the principle round which to rally and save her from the ills of anarchy and disunion.

This is the course of English history, and many of its peculiarities may be derived from the fact that feudalism was introduced in so modified a form by William the Conqueror. To sum up what has been said. In France the crown began in weakness and ended in despotism. In England it began in strength and ended in a limited monarchy.

The importance of ecclesiastical history in early times is very great. The ecclesiastics were not only the spiritual teachers of the people, the moral, social, educational organisers of society: they were the statesmen, the lawyers, the diplomatists, the writers, architects, even sometimes the warriors of the times. The Church was the real avenue to power and influence in every department of intellectual life, the only avenue for poor but able men. Elsewhere the path was hedged up by the privileges of an aristocracy; here they found scope for their genius and ambition, and rose with rapid strides by mere force of mind to the highest positions of the state. When to this is added the influence of the monasteries, which has already been mentioned, it will be clear that there was absolutely no department of active life which the Church did not interpenetrate and in which churchmen did not take the lead. The Church was 'an all-pervading and animating energy, quickening the whole social and political system, and formed the intellectual starting-point of the age.'

It was therefore most necessary that William should turn his attention to the improvement of the Anglo-Saxon Church. Much moreover was needed. At the time of the Norman Conquest, the Anglo-Saxon Church, after having contributed not a little to the growth of national unity, and given its aid in the local organisation of the country, had fallen somewhat behind the standard of the time. The discipline, the morals, and the intelligence of the secular clergy had been relaxed; most of them were married, contrary to the opinions of those days, and there was even danger of their becoming a close hereditary caste, holding their possessions as so much family property descending from father to son, and thereby forgetting the trust character of the Church's revenues. It had been mainly with the view of reforming the English Church and drawing it closer to Rome that the Pope had sanctioned the expedition of William. The question was, how far would William comply?

To understand clearly the meaning of William's reforms in this respect, it is necessary to say a few words on the great ecclesiastical system of Gregory VII., who at this time sat on the papal throne.

Feudalism, the first definite scheme after the fall of the empire of Charlemagne for organising political society, had hopelessly failed. The only possible means by which it could have succeeded was by maintaining intact the mutual duties of over-lord, under-lord, vassal, and villein. These once destroyed, feudalism became a mere excuse for perpetual quarrels between the barons and for intolerable oppression of the despised non-military classes. All cohesion in the European state-system was destroyed, and society and government, except under the temporary rule of some great man, were little more than a legalised anarchy.

Europe, cursed by this system, 'was losing all knowledge of its own unity, all strength, and rapidly drifting into meaningless, pitiless antagonism of nations, classes, and individuals.' It was from the clergy, or rather from the monasteries, that the opposition to this state of things arose. From the monasteries the impulse was communicated to the bishops, and from the bishops to the popes, who take up the work and try to give it principle and organisation.

During the ninth century the papacy had fallen a victim to the evils abroad, and sank in degradation and contempt. Raised in the tenth century from this degradation by Otho I, and his successors she rapidly regained lost ground under the 'German popes,' and rose daily to higher aspirations, to culminate in the accession of Gregory VII. This man, under his name of Hildebrand, had long held an important position in Europe. Son of a Tuscan carpenter, he had early embraced monasticism, and as a monk of Clugny, in Burgundy, had subjected himself to the discipline of the Benedictine rule. Returning to Rome, he became the great pope-maker of his day, contributed to the election of five of his predecessors, and directed the papal policy. On the death of Alexander II. (1073), the papal tiara, to which he had never aspired, was laid at his feet, and, abandoning the seclusion of monastic life, he ascended the papal throne, prepared to subdue the world in the same spirit in which he had hitherto striven to conquer himself. Under Gregory VII. the schemes which had steadily been growing were perfected, and monasticism in his election rose to her highest fortune.

Gregory VII., seeing the conflicting principles at work in Europe, the chaotic confusion, the triumph of cruelty and disorder, conceived the magnificent idea of a great spiritual autocracy which should serve as a principle of unity round which Europe might gather, and a force which should join together rival classes and interests. The Pope was to be the supreme head of Christendom, and ultimate arbiter of her affairs. To him should all appeals be made on international questions, on questions of peace and war; while within the states his authority should watch over the inferior courts and see justice done. Elsewhere violence and fraud might run riot, but here, at Rome at least, all questions should be decided on the highest grounds of equity and morality. Other tribunals might be open only to the rich and powerful; here all should gain a hearing. Elsewhere wickedness in high places might escape punishment, but here morality should be enforced on kings as well as on subjects, and the proudest criminal reduced to submission.

Thus might the 'truce of God' in time extend all over Europe, and wars be made to cease. Thus might the weak find aid against the strong, and right maintain itself against might; while Europe, united in the confession of one faith, might here see reflected the image of its unity and its majesty.

This magnificent ideal, it has been well said, was crossed by human frailty even in Gregory's days. 'Subsequently it was fatally degraded and discredited by the selfish and faithless temporising, the shameless greediness which grew into proverbs, wherever the name of Rome was mentioned. It was maintained by shameful means and shameless forgeries which escaped detection from the uncritical eye of Europe at that time. The power grew to be abused, to usurp the powers to which it was to have served as a counterpoise. It went through the usual course of successful power in human hands, and in every succeeding century these things grew worse. The ideal became more and more a shadow, the reality a more corrupt and intolerable mockery. But still it remains the most magnificent failure in human history.'

Such was the ideal conceived, and partly realised, by Gregory VII. Let us consider what was necessary to its realisation. First, the sovereigns of Europe must be induced, if possible, to do homage to the Pope, for naturally the scheme took the feudal shape which then predominated, and without such subordination the scheme could not work. Then, the celibacy of the clergy must be enforced, whereby they might become a separate order freed from secular interests and connected closely with the Pope.

The ecclesiastical courts in each separate state must be made independent of the secular, and secured in their jurisdiction over all clerks and all causes affecting morality and religion. Lay *investiture* (investing the bishop with the ring and the crozier) must be condemned, lest the clergy should become dependent upon the secular arm, and simony and servility enervate them. Thus the clergy, bound to the Pope by the ties of interest and devotion, would be a ready instrument in his hand for carrying out his schemes.

These were the principles of Gregory's plan, which he was vigorously pressing upon Europe, and which he now hoped to see carried out in England.

William was not unwilling in most respects to satisfy his wishes. His policy may for clearness be classed under two heads: (1) The relation of the Church to the State; (2) The relation of Church and State to Rome.

(1) In Anglo-Saxon times the Church and State had been closely connected. The bishops had sat side by side with the secular officers in the Shire court. The Witenagemot had been as much an ecclesiastical as a secular assembly; its laws, indeed, had been rather ecclesiastical canons than secular laws. This William altered. Fully aware of the importance of the Church as a department of State, as a principle of order, he conceived the idea of using it as a counterbalance to the feudal barons, ever ready

to overthrow the central authority of the crown, and establish their own selfish independence. Hence his first care was to reform the Church and increase its power.

Stigand, the Archbishop of Canterbury, convicted of illegally holding the See of Winchester with his own archbishopric, and of having received the pallium, the symbol of his metropolitan power, from the false pope, Benedict X., was removed, and most of the Anglo-Saxon bishops shared his fate. In their place William sought Europe over for worthy substitutes. Lanfranc, called from Normandy, where he had been made abbot of William's monastery of St. Stephen at Caen, was appointed archbishop, and under him the reform was continued. The supremacy of Canterbury over York was asserted. Marriage of the clergy was discouraged; the already married clergy were tolerated, but future marriages were strictly prohibited. In the chapters monks were substituted for the secular canons. The monasteries were reformed according to the stricter rules of the Norman monasteries to which Lanfranc had been accustomed.

Having thus reformed the worst abuses of the Church, William proceeded to increase its power. Two of the bishops, Durham and Kent, were entrusted with Counties Palatine. Many of the village bishops were removed into fortified towns that they might be better able to resist the feudal nobles. The see of Lichfield was removed to Chester, Sherborne to Salisbury, Selsey to Chichester, Dorchester in Oxfordshire to Lincoln. The leading clergy were called to William's councils, and frequently were appointed to the office of justiciary and others, while the chancellor was invariably an ecclesiastic.

Lastly, William removed the bishop from the county court, and erected ecclesiastical courts in each diocese. In these the bishop alone presided over all cases which affected the spiritual or Church interests.

(2) So far William fell in with Gregory's scheme, and reorganised the English Church. But this was not all that Gregory claimed. He demanded the homage of the king. This William would not grant. Friendly relations with Rome he was anxious to maintain, and the tax of Peter's Pence he would gladly pay; he would even acknowledge the general supremacy of the Pope. But the oath of homage he would not take, 'for neither,' said he, 'had he ever promised so to do, nor had his predecessors done so,' and Gregory, anxious to secure his friendship, dared not press the question of Investiture.

The general character of his policy is summed up in the so-called Customs. By these he ordered that the king's leave must be obtained before any Pope were acknowledged in England, before any papal synod were held, any letter of the Pope's received, before any bishop appealed to Rome, or any tenant in capite (those who held their lands immediately of the king) were excommunicated.

Thus William clearly showed himself determined to rule the Church of England, and against the great scheme of Gregory VII. asserted a contrary one, that of a National Church, owing, indeed, a nominal allegiance to Rome, closely assimilated to her in doctrine, ritual and organization, but still absolutely under the power of the crown.

In all this William was heartily supported by the vigorous common-sense of Lanfranc, and Gregory had his hands too full in pressing his claims on the Emperor, Henry IV., to quarrel with William on the subject.

Thus, during William's time, the system was firmly established, and no quarrel arose till the reigns of his successors.

The policy of William, it can hardly be doubted, was on the whole beneficial. The abuses of the Anglo-Saxon Church were removed. Norman bishops were certainly better educated, and it was well that the Church should be brought into closer connexion with Rome, which, with all its faults, was the real source of vigour at that date. Under their influence the activity of the Church revived, while her discipline was improved.

In the increased power of the Church a valuable balance was found to that of the feudal baronage, while the Church itself was kept in check by the unqualified authority of the king.

In all these way's William's changes were for good, but in two ways they did harm.

(1) The right of royal patronage, though fairly administered by William, was under his immediate successor shamefully abused; and (2) in William's ordinance erecting the spiritual courts lay the foundation of many a serious quarrel in after times. His error here is to be found, not so much in erecting the courts, as in not more clearly defining the limits of their jurisdiction. During his own reign this caused no difficulty, but very soon the ecclesiastical courts began to encroach upon the temporal. In these encroachments the churchmen were not indeed actuated entirely by selfish motives, or by narrow professional motives. Owing to the

more perfect system of procedure established in their courts, they became exceedingly popular and people flocked of their own accord to the bishop's court. But the result was most pernicious. The jurisdiction of the ecclesiastical courts grew apace, and infringed on that of the temporal. The clergy's privilege of being tried by these courts alone threatened to render them absolutely independent of the secular arm, and finally, under Henry II. the abuses were so flagrant that Henry interfered, and fought his fatal quarrel with Becket on this very point.

CHAPTER XIV.
END OF REIGN OF WILLIAM I.

We must now return to the year 1071, the date of the final conquest of the country, William was not fated to enjoy a lengthened peace, and no sooner were the Anglo-Saxon revolts crushed than troubles arose from different quarters.

The conquest of Maine had been accomplished just before William's invasion of England; but his rule was most distasteful to the people of that province and they now took the opportunity of his absence to abandon their allegiance. They first appealed to one of the daughters of their last Count, Herbert, who came north with her husband, Azzo Marquis of Este, and occupied the country. This, however, did not satisfy the townsmen of Le Mans, the capital. They had long suffered from the arbitrary rule of their petty feudal lords, and were anxious to establish their liberties on some more secure basis. Accordingly they formed themselves into a municipality or commune, bound themselves to maintain their new-born freedom, and again fell back upon their old overlord the Count of Anjou, who thus once more ruled in Maine.

The news at once brought William across the Channel. Fulk was tardy in his assistance, and the rebels, to escape the wasting of their lands, surrendered the town, and acknowledged Robert, William's eldest son, as their Count. Still, William dared not crush out the spirit of municipal freedom. He promised to observe their privileges, and Le Mans, losing her independence, retained her civic rights, to become one of the earliest privileged communes of Northern France.

At the treaty of Blanchelande which followed between Fulk and William, Robert consented to hold the County as a fief of Anjou.

From this petty quarrel on the Continent William was recalled by an outbreak of his feudal barons at home. Their rebellion opens a new phase of English history. It was the first of those attempts on the part of the feudal nobles to throw off the stern rule of their new-found kings which troubled England till the reign of Henry II.

The actual companions of William in his invasion had submitted to him; but they were now fast dying out, and it is their sons who now rebel against the stern rule of the Conqueror. The Earldom of Hereford was now in the hands of Roger de Breteuil, the son of William's trusted adviser and justiciary William Fitz-Osbern; that of Norfolk was in the hands of Ralph Guader. These two earls, in common with many of the Norman nobles, had long chafed under the strict rule of William, and longed to establish their feudal independence in England.

William, moreover, had forbidden a marriage between Ralph and Roger's sister, probably because he feared the result of such an alliance. This filled up the measure of their discontent. In spite of William's refusal, they solemnised the marriage. At the bridal feast they entered into a conspiracy, and gained the assistance of Waltheof Earl of Northampton, the only remaining Anglo-Saxon earl, who had been treated kindly by William, and given the king's niece Judith in marriage. Their intentions are clearly seen from the agreement made between them. England was to be restored to the condition it was in during King Edward's reign. One of the three conspirators should be king, the other two earls, who of course would enjoy practical independence. The attempt, however, entirely failed. The Anglo-Saxons knew their interests too well to join the rebellion, and it was speedily suppressed. Ralph fled to Brittany, and Roger was taken prisoner to end his days in captivity. The fate of Waltheof was more tragic. It does not appear that he gave more than a tacit acquiescence to the conspiracy. Indeed, when the rebellion broke out he betrayed the plot to Lanfranc, and was for the moment pardoned. But soon after the accusation was again revived, and he was put to death, some said at the instigation of his unnatural wife. This, the only political execution of William's reign, has been bitterly laid to his account. It was cruel, it was perhaps hardly just; but no doubt William was prompted to the act by political motives. It was an act of policy to destroy the last chief of the Anglo-Saxon race, the last leader to whom they could look. But Waltheof was looked upon as a national saint by the conquered people, and the later troubles of William's reign were by them considered as the vengeance of God upon the king's tyranny.

For here the prosperity of William's reign ceased. Hitherto he had been successful in all his wars and in every scheme he undertook. From this date failures began to thicken around him, while his character darkened as life drew to a close. His temper waxed harsher, his yoke lay heavier on his subjects, his craving for money grew, and England suffered greatly.

Next year followed the revolt of his son Robert, which again assumed the character of a rebellion of the feudal nobles. Before invading England William had promised to resign Normandy to his eldest son in the event of his success. This he probably did to allay the jealousy of Philip of France; but it was only a nominal promise, and when Robert claimed its fulfilment, William curtly answered that 'he did not intend to throw off his clothes till he went to bed.' On this, Robert rose in arms, and was aided by Philip of France, and many of the young nobility, who seized the opportunity once more to establish their independence. Robert of Belesme, son of Roger Montgomery of Shrewsbury, and William of Breteuil, son of William Fitz-Osbern, and brother of the old conspirator Roger, were the two most important men, both sons of William's most trusted advisers. In the action which ensued at Gerberoi, William, unhorsed and wounded by his son, was forced to seek a reconciliation, to which Robert, who was struck with horror at his own deed, consented.

William's half-brother Odo next disturbed the realm. To this man, Bishop of Bayeux, had been given the County Palatine of Kent. But even this did not satisfy his ambitious spirit. He aimed at becoming Pope, and prepared an army in England to enforce his claim. His turbulent and cruel conduct had long caused trouble to William, and now he was arrested. This arrest might have been considered an encroachment on the privileges of ecclesiastics, who claimed to be tried in their own courts granted them by William himself. William, therefore, declared him arrested not as bishop but as earl, and did not release him till he himself was on his death-bed.

In 1085 William was threatened by danger from another quarter. The Kings of Norway and Denmark had looked with jealousy upon the success of the Norman William. Olaf of Norway might still have remembered the compact between Tostig and Harald Hardrada, while Canute, who then ruled in Denmark, though allied by marriage with William through his wife, the daughter of Robert le Frison, Count of Flanders, had already made settlements in England. Canute now prepared for a last attempt, and, gaining the aid of Olaf and of the Count of Flanders, threatened William with a formidable coalition. William, to meet the danger, hastily levied foreign mercenaries, and, to secure the fidelity of his subjects, exacted the famous oath of homage from all his subjects at the Council of Sarum. Fortunately, however, the expedition was checked by contrary winds. Olaf was bribed by William, and in the following year Canute fell a victim to a rebellion of his own subjects, caused by discontent at his hasty innovations. From this time the Danes lost the command of the sea. The reforms inaugurated by Canute brought their institutions into conformity with the rest of Europe, and Denmark troubled her no more.

The Danish invasion probably hastened the completion of the Domesday Survey, one of the most important acts of William's reign. This great work completes the organization of

William. (1.) It was intended to serve as the basis of taxation; (2) as the authority by which all disputes concerning land might be settled; (3) and as a muster roll of the nation. As a census it is not exhaustive; the three northern counties and part of Westmorland, Lancashire, and Monmouthshire, probably on account of their disturbed state, are not mentioned, nor are London and Winchester and a few other towns, probably because of charters of immunity previously granted. But as far as it goes it is very exact and correct. From its pages the Conqueror could at a glance discover the state of his revenues, the wealth, the consequence of every personage in his kingdom. No nation in Europe possesses such a monument of its early state, nor can later times point to many achievements like it. The means by which the information was to be collected were these. Commissioners went forth into every shire, and there, calling the sheriffs, the parish priests, the reeves of the townships, and men of each manor before them, required them on their oath to answer these questions: 'What is the name of your township? Who was lord thereof, bishop or abbot in the days of Good King Edward? How many thanes, how many freemen, how many villeins are there? How many acres, and what their value in King Edward's time? What their value now? What has each freeman? How many oxen, how many cows, how many sheep, how many swine? 'The information thus collected was then put into shape, and called the Domesday Book, and with such activity was the work carried on that it was completed within a year. Loud were the complaints throughout the land, and in some places riots ensued. The people considered it an arbitrary invasion of their rights. It is a shame, they said, that the king should pry into each man's means, a shame even to tell of such tyranny, though the king thought no shame to do it. Such is always the cry of the opponents of order, and the independence of the English resented, as they have ever done, the interference of government. But their complaints were ill-founded. It was no tyranny, but the work of a great organization, the essential preliminary and accompaniment of strong government. On its completion a great assembly was held in Salisbury Plain, when the ordinance before mentioned was passed, ordering every freeman to take an oath of allegiance directly to the king himself.

In the following year a quarrel broke out with Philip for the possession of the Vexin. This had been granted by Henry I. to William's father in return for the aid given by the Norman duke to Henry when fighting for his crown. But Philip now invaded it. William, irritated by a coarse jest of the French king, ravaged the country and burnt the town of Mantes. As he proudly rode over the ruins of the town, his horse stumbled on some hot ashes, and the rider, thrown violently on the pommel, sustained a fatal injury. Carried to Rouen, he lingered long enough to declare his wishes. Robert was given Normandy and the lands which William had gained by inheritance.

William Rufus, his second son, he named as successor to those lands which he had gained himself, while to Henry, his third son, he left a present of 5,000 pounds of silver, with the prophetic promise that he, becoming greater than either of his brothers, would one day possess far greater and ampler power. Then turning to his confessor, he deplored the evils of his past life. ^ No tongue can tell,' said he, 'the deeds of wickedness I have perpetrated in my weary pilgrimage of toil and care.' He deplored his birth: born to warfare, polluted with bloodshed from his earliest years, his trials, the base ingratitude he had met with. He also extolled his own virtues, praised his conscientious appointments in the Church and his alms, and then, freeing all the state captives with a prophecy of the ills that Odo by his ambition would bring upon his country, passed away at the hour of prime. Thus the great Conqueror was at last at rest.

The scene of his death was a sad satire on the power of man. His sons, eager only to gain their appointed shares, departed before their father's eyes were closed—Rufus to England, Robert to Normandy, Henry to seize the treasure; and the corpse of the strong man who but a few minutes before struck fear into all who angered him, was now shamefully despoiled and stripped, and hurried, almost without decent burial, into its unkingly grave, the owner of the soil demanding his price before he allowed the body to be buried.

A great man thus passed away—a man who did great things for England. In William the Norman character found its greatest representative. To the consummate powers of a general he added the subtle skill of a diplomatist and the foresight of a statesman. Born a bastard, and left fatherless at an early age, he triumphed over all his foes in Normandy, and strongly organized his dukedom. Then passing from Normandy to England, he changed the name of Bastard for that of Conqueror, and in welding the Saxon and Norman institutions together he illustrated the Norman talent for adaptation by his wise and thoughtful policy. He reorganized our whole political life, saved England from the ills which were eating at its core, gave it unity and strength, and first made it a great power in Europe. Yet these great qualities of his were stained by great blemishes. William was an irresponsible despot, and his people found him so. To the Anglo-Saxons, although he continued the old national and constitutional forms, and left to the people the enjoyment of their own law, he was stark and stern. The form of their government remained, but the spirit was changed, and many are the complaints on account of the fiscal and other oppressions. His rule was that of a wise and wary, a strong and resolute, an arbitrary though not a wanton despot. He marked out his goal, and no scruples of conscience or mercy stayed him from attaining it. There was nothing which he would not do to gain his end, and much was the suffering he thereby brought on both Anglo-Saxon and Norman. He was a man born to be feared, not to be loved, and when life had departed, and the great Conqueror's hand lay cold, the indignities which mean wretches heaped upon the lifeless corpse bore witness to the fact that fear once gone, hatred arose and drove out even the sentiment of respect.

CHAPTER XV.
WILLIAM RUFUS.

In the separation of England from Normandy, according to the will of the Conqueror, we have a clue to the reign of William Rufus and many a succeeding reign. The English welcomed that act as a restoration of their nationality, and a pledge that England should no longer be a mere province of the Norman kingdom. Headed, therefore, by Lanfranc, who had imbibed thoroughly English sympathies, and Wulfstan, Bishop of Worcester, the only national bishop who remained, they heartily supported the claims of William Rufus, and welcomed his coronation at Winchester with delight. The Norman baronage, on the contrary, resented the separation of the two kingdoms, whereby their conquered possessions in England were separated from their hereditary property in Normandy, and their hopes of establishing their feudal independence were marred. Led by Odo of Bayeux and the Count of Mortain, both half-brothers of the Conqueror, Roger of Montgomery, and his son Robert of Belesme, Eustace of Boulogne, and Roger Bigod, they disputed the will of the Conqueror, and supported the claim of Robert.

Rufus was thus forced to appeal to the English. He issued a proclamation, in which he promised to refrain from arbitrary taxations, to give up all newly introduced abuses, and to let everyone sport on his own domain. Then summoning all the English to join him, on pain of being proclamied *nithing* or worthless, he collected an army to which London and the Cinque Ports largely contributed. He reduced the castle of Rochester, which Odo had seized, bought off Roger Montgomery of Shrewsbury, and drove the rebels from the country.

He then leagued himself with the discontented nobles of Normandy and invaded that duchy, until he was bought off by Robert, who consented to a treaty by which the survivor was to succeed to the other's dominions if either died without heirs.

Rufus was thus established on the English throne entirely through the assistance of the English. They were ill requited by the oppressive tyrant. As long as Lanfranc lived he was restrained by his influence; but when Lanfranc died his true character began to show itself. With much of the ability, decision, and good generalship of his father, he presented in other respects a complete contrast to him. William I., in spite of his many faults, had been at heart a religious and austere man. He had hated anarchy as dangerous to his realm, and licentiousness as the outward garb of anarchy. His son was utterly wanting in all religious principle, and shocked the morals even of that age by his boisterous and indecent profligacy. His abilities were prostituted to his selfish love of power, and instead of trying to prevent anarchy in his kingdom, he turned it to his own account. Wanting in the business-like qualities of his father, he entrusted all state matters to his minister, Ranulf Flambard, who resembled the son much as Lanfranc resembled the father. If Lanfranc was the best of the statesmen ecclesiastics, Ranulf Flambard was the worst. Born of a low Norman family, which had settled in the New Forest under Edward the Confessor, he became one of the clerks of the Chancery, rapidly rose to favour, and became Bishop of Durham and chief minister. Now was seen the result of the great authority assumed by William over the Church, and how by a wicked king that power might be abused; and England experienced all the ills to avoid which the papal idea been formed. Ranulf Flambard was one of those churchmen who had become entirely secularised by the drudgery of the Chancery business, and, now in power, he proceeded to let those secular ideas have full play. Without education, but with great natural powers and boundless fluency of tongue, coarse, impudent, and cunning, he was just the servant for the infamous Rufus. Abetted by the king, he ground down the people by fiscal oppression, and then deliberately set to work not only to plunder but to degrade and injure the Church. He introduced a system of barefaced and daring venality, which put up everything in Church and State for sale, .and threatened to secularise the Church itself. He started the theory that the vacant benefices belonged to the king, following the analogy of the temporal fiefs. For years after Lanfranc's death the See of Canterbury was kept vacant, and its revenues were dissipated in contributing to the dissolute tastes of the king, who declared that no one should be archbishop but himself. In this policy the Red king was influenced by two motives—first, to free himself from the irksome restraint which an archbishop would be sure to place upon his gross and reckless profligacy; and secondly, because he knew that so long as the primacy was vacant, little opposition would be offered to him, and he would find it easy to wreak his will upon the rest of the possessions of the Church. So steadily was this perverse policy maintained, that at the end of his reign not only was the archbishop of Canterbury an exile, but four bishoprics and eleven abbeys were without pastors. In the struggle, the bishops, jealous of the supremacy of Canterbury, showed singular apathy. Thus, in spite of the discontent of his people and the frequent petitions to him, one of which is peculiar, 'that the king would allow it to be enjoined that the people should pray that the king's heart might be changed, he continued obstinate until a dangerous illness brought on a temporary fit of remorse as violent as is usual in ill-balanced minds. Then, at last, giving way to a long-expressed desire of his country, he appointed Anselm Archbishop of Canterbury.

This great man was a Lombard, like Lanfranc, and of noble birth. He had been attracted to Bec by the fame of Lanfranc, and there, in spite of their very different characters, had become one of his dearest friends. To his predecessor he formed a complete contrast. Lanfranc was a man of the world, gifted with a practical, vigorous turn of mind. Anselm, on the contrary, deficient in the worldly qualities, far surpassed his friend in originality of thought and subtlety of mind. He was the first great philosopher of Christian Europe, and in his works at once laid the basis of the future scholastic philosophy, and went beyond it. Eager for the discovery of exact truth, he plunged fearlessly into the great questions of the proof of the existence of God, the relation of faith to reason, the meaning of the Incarnation—subjects which after him were scarcely touched till the fifteenth and sixteenth centuries. His biographer and friend, Eadmer, tells us of the astonishment caused by his attempts to unravel 'these the darkest of the questions concerning the Divine Nature and our faith, which lay hid or covered by much obscurity in the Divine Scriptures.' To this speculative turn of mind Anselm added a childlike simplicity, a tenderness never surpassed. He loved to teach the young and to mould their minds when 'they were still like wax, ready to take the impression marked upon them.' 'He loved to tend the sick, and he behaved,' says his chronicler, 'so that all men loved him as their dear father. He so touched the hearts of the English that there was no count or countess or powerful person but thought they had lost much in the sight of God if it had not chanced to them to have done some service to him. So it was, he was to those in health a father, to the sick a mother.' Even the stern Conqueror William loved him better than any man, and wished to see him before anyone else when he lay on his death-bed. Yet with all this tenderness he was austere; inexorably severe to his own faults and to those of others, and, once convinced that any course was wrong, no power on earth could make him acquiesce in it.

After Lanfranc had been removed to St. Stephen's at Caen, Anselm had become abbot of Bec, and now he was called to succeed him in the See of Canterbury. This he accepted very much against his will, and only from the highest sense of duty, upon William making three promises: (1) To acknowledge Urban II. pope; (2) To restore all property belonging to the See of Canterbury; (3) To act on the advice and counsel of the archbishop.

The ills which might ensue from the subservience of the Church to the king had clearly appeared during the past few years, and must have furnished proof to Anselm of the dangers of the System. England thereby was in danger of again being cut off from Rome, and of having its Church reduced to the condition of a mere slave to the king, who could despoil it of its revenues at will. It would have thus lost all independence, have become degraded, and, losing all moral consistency of purpose, would have ceased to struggle against immorality and wickedness, or to influence the country for good. But Anselm scarcely needed such argument. For, as if by poetic justice, Rufus could not have appointed a more resolute antagonist. Lanfranc was the representative of the independence of the national church. Anselm was the supporter of the papal authority in its extremest pretensions. Deficient in the strong practical common-sense which characterised his predecessor, he was by his contemplative, imaginative character better fitted to find rest in a great ideal, to which his philosophical spirit would give an existence and a reality which it did not, in fact, possess. Lanfranc was a thorough man of the world, and saw the dangers of the papal scheme, and how it failed in the; working. Anselm was in no sort a man of the world, but a speculative recluse, a man of books and thought, and was carried away by the magnificence of the scheme which promised to complete the gradation of the hierarchy and give completeness and sanctity to the whole feudal society. The whole world might be considered as holding of one another, and all eventually of the Pope, who himself, as his vicegerent, held of Christ. Thus all the world might be considered the vassals and servants of Christ, in theory as well as in fact. Was not this worth struggling for 1 Such were the thoughts of the man whom William Rufus had placed in the archiepiscopal chair.

The result might have been easily foreseen. The archbishop at once claimed the fulfilment of the promises made when he accepted the primacy. He reproved the vices of the royal court, where the king, with his renewed health, had retaken to his old courses, and where the licentious ways of the courtiers, their effeminate dress, long hair, and peaked shoes, did violence to Anselm's pious character. He attacked the king for keeping benefices vacant, and refusing to restore the property alienated from the See of Canterbury. William, on his part, demanded a gift from his See. This Anselm, not improperly, refused, because a simoniacal interpretation might be put upon the transaction, and it would inevitably lead to simony,

The question of investiture next came forward. The grant of the 'pallium,' or ecclesiastical vestment symbolical of metropolitan authority, had been claimed by the Popes since the investiture, sixth century, and Anselm now asked leave to go to Rome to obtain it. William refused with anger, declaring that he had not even yet accepted Urban II., who was struggling against an anti-pope, and he claimed the right of acknowledging the Pope or no as he pleased. He even thought of deposing Anselm, and in this was supported by the bishops, who showed strange servility. But the common-sense of the barons checked him, and the matter was settled by a compromise. Urban, struggling as he was with the emperor, Henry IV., on the same question, dared not press his claims on England, and when William acknowledged him, allowed the pallium to be laid on the altar rails, whence Anselm took it and invested himself. But there could be no truce between archbishop and king; and finally, when Rufus accused Anselm of sending his contingent improperly armed to the Welsh war then going on, Anselm demanded leave to go to Rome to consult the Pope. William seized the opportunity of freeing himself from his archbishop. He bade him go, but never more return; and for the rest of the king's life the See of Canterbury was kept practically vacant, and the revenues were appropriated by the king. Thus began that system of appeals to Rome, which became so fruitful of future ills. Yet in all this Anselm was so clearly fighting for what was right, that our sympathies are entirely with him, and we are only too glad to forgive any slight temper or want of tact and courtesy which at times appear in him. He was not, indeed, fitted to battle with the world, with the overbearing insolence and noisy tyranny of a wanton despot like William Rufus. Eadmer, his loving chronicler, most pathetically illustrates this: 'We were accustomed to lead him away from the assembly a little when he was tired, and restore him with a passage of Scripture or a theological question. We asked him why he, such a vigorous man, became on such occasions so weak and faint-hearted. He replied that in this respect; he was altogether a child. He likened himself to an owl who is only well when it is with its young ones in its hole, but if it comes out among the crows and ravens sees nothing but pecking beaks and knows not which way to turn.' Nor again are we inclined to be scrupulous even on questions where principle was at stake, such as the question of the pallium, which affected the principle of the royal supremacy; or, again, Anselm's demand to go to Rome for advice, whereby he had broken, so his cruel oppressor asserted, William the Conqueror's 'customs.' The question of principle we postpone to Henry I.'s reign, when it comes forward more prominently. During the quarrel with Rufus it is overborne by other questions. William Rufus was a violent, unscrupulous, and rapacious tyrant, the very man against whom the Pope had raised his scheme; and Anselm, after having most unwillingly accepted the archiepiscopal office, resolutely stood up for the good and right and just. Indeed, we go as far as to say that had all kings been like Rufus, all archbishops like Anselm, the papal authority could not have been pressed too strongly, or the ecclesiastical censures wielded too severely. The existence of such kings, of such brutality, selfishness, and misrule, justifies the extremest of the papal claims. And, lastly, it is important to remember that in this opposition of the Church to the irresponsible despotism of the Norman kings, the people first learnt their right and duty to resist an encroaching royal power, a lesson which they had else easily forgotten.

During the quarrel with Anselm the following events had happened.

Malcolm Canmore, brought up in the court of Edward the Confessor, had overthrown the usurper Macbeth in 1054, through the aid of Siward of Northumbria. This English alliance was subsequently strengthened by his marriage with Margaret, sister of Edgar the Ætheling.

Accordingly, during William's reign, Malcolm had supported the national revolts against the Conqueror, but had been defeated and forced to swear allegiance to William. He still, however, continued his English policy, and his court formed the chief refuge for the English when flying from Norman tyranny. Thus the English language and institutions spread to Scotland, and the latter became the basis of the Scotch constitution. Feudalism was established. The Lothians, Anglicised by the recoil of the Norman invasion, were thoroughly civilised, and under Malcolm began to form the nucleus of the future Scottish kingdom. The discipline and ceremonial of the English Church were introduced, to improve the condition of the Keltic Church, which had become disorganized. English clergy were sent by Lanfranc, and monasteries after the Norman model were established.

In 1091 hostilities broke out once more between the two countries. The quarrel was at first compromised by Malcolm doing homage to William, but two years afterwards Malcolm complained of William's conduct in fortifying Carlisle and settling English peasants from the south there. This he asserted to be a violation of the rights of the Scotch king, who claimed

Cumberland as immediate lord. On William's refusal to do him justice, Malcolm invaded the northern counties, but, when he was besieging Alnwick, was surprised by Robert Mowbray, Earl of Northumberland, and slain. Margaret died soon after, and Scotland became the victim of a civil war. The Keltic population, who had been jealous of the English sympathies of Malcolm and the supremacy of Lothian, followed Donald Bean, the brother of Malcolm, who also gained the support of Magnus of Norway; while Malcolm's children led the English party. This war was not ended till the year 1097, when Edgar, the son of Margaret, was restored by Edgar the Ætheling, with the help of an English army lent him by William. Under this king the Anglicising process became complete, and Scotland became, at some little distance behind, the counterpart of England.

Meanwhile Rufus had been engaged in crushing another rebellion of his feudal nobles headed by Mowbray, Earl of Northumberland, and in another war with Robert. On this occasion he ordered a general levy of the militia to the coast, and then, exacting ten shillings from each, the journey-money they had received from their counties, sent them home again. This extortion helped to fill his treasury, but the war was not carried on; and shortly afterwards Robert, eager to join the first Crusade, pledged Normandy to his brother for the sum of 6,666*l*.

In the Crusade which followed but few of William's subjects took part. It was not till the second Crusade that England caught the enthusiasm of the Continent, and joined the rest of Europe in her great wars against the East. But many a Norman noble followed Robert, to join their cousins of the South on the shores of Palestine, and the fortunes of the first Crusade are so closely bound up with the Norman name that it calls for a passing notice here.

To understand the causes of the Crusades we must remember the many conflicting emotions which stirred the heart of Europe, and which, for once united in the Crusades, hurled Western Europe upon Asia.

These causes, as far as the masses were concerned, were mainly two.

(1) A spirit of religious enthusiasm. This, taking as was natural in those days an outward material form, had caused that great monastic revival of which we have before spoken, and had led many pilgrims along the weary and dangerous road to Palestine. The fascination of the Holy Land was irresistible. Men could not believe that there was not some real tangible virtue in the Holy Land itself. Would not the mere standing on the ground hallowed by the scenes of their Lord's life and death at once purge them from the pollution of their sins and make them clean? Thus, as we draw near to the era of the Crusades, there is hardly a king, a duke, a count, who had not been on a pilgrimage to the holy places, or had not died lamenting that death had cut him off ere his vow had been fulfilled. This was the spirit which was lashed to religious frenzy by the

news that Jerusalem had fallen into the hands of the Turks (1096), that the pilgrims were cruelly treated, and that the Sepulchre of our Lord, hitherto respected even by Mahometans, was treated with contempt.

(2) There was that spirit of adventure, which, often degenerating into reckless licence, alone explains the anarchy of the times. In the Crusade men saw for the first time the possibility of satisfying these strangely divergent passions, and hence in part the extraordinary enthusiasm which seized on Western Christendom. Hitherto these discordant impulses had conflicted and had caused the strange contrasts marking the lives of the men of the earlier ages—cruelty and rapacity alternating with strange fits of terrified devotion. A life spent in wild licence suddenly hid in the obscurity of a monastery; men expiating past misdeeds by frantic efforts of self-abasement.

But among the leaders these simple motives were supplemented and sometimes obscured by others. The Pope saw in the crusades the only hope of a great coalition against the infidel foe. The Turkish hosts were threatening Europe, and if not checked in time the struggle might have to be fought out in Europe itself. Europe, unconscious as she was of her unity, knew not how to coalesce. The Church alone formed a bond of union, and the only hope of united action lay in a religious war. So thought Gregory VII. himself, and he had tried to preach a Crusade before his death. To this view, in the case of Urban II., was added the imperative necessity of gaining the aid of Europe against his rival the anti-pope, set up by his enemy the Emperor Henry IV.; and how could this be better done than by preaching a crusade, and thus assuming the leadership of the great Christian army, whose designs, it might be said, the Emperor was thwarting by his own selfish aims? The commercial towns of Italy looked to these Crusades in the hope of re-establishing their commerce with the East, which had been endangered by the fall of

Jerusalem, at that time the market for Eastern goods. But, lastly, the counts and feudal lords of Europe hoped to carve principalities for themselves out of the wealthy East. We have mentioned a few of the many causes which led to the Crusades, because these alone explain the strange unanimity which for once seized Europe. For the rest we must content ourselves with dwelling on the influence of the Normans upon the first Crusade.

No king or emperor joined the first Crusade. It was rather a war of counts and dukes. Viewed from this aspect, it assumes the appearance of a great family coalition, and divides into four leading interests.

(1) The Lorraine and Flemish interest, headed by Godfrey of Bouillon, Duke of Lorraine; Robert, Count of Flanders; and Baldwin of Hainault, his cousin.

(2) The Vermandois party, headed by Hugh of Vermandois, brother of Philip, King of France, who, through his marriage with Adela, heiress of the old Counts of Vermandois, was

closely connected with the Lorraine and Flemish interests.

(3) The Norman party, headed by Bohemond, Prince of Tarento; Tancred, his cousin; and Robert, Duke of Normandy.

All these were more or less united by ties of blood and interest. The Counts of Flanders were connected with the ducal houses of Normandy and Apulia by marriage; with the houses of Boulogne and Vermandois by the tie of sympathy. The house of Boulogne had long had dealings with the Normans of England. Eustace, the father of the Crusader, had been one of the Normanising party under Edward the Confessor, then a rebel under William I. Eustace, this man's son, had joined Robert against William Rufus, and was eventually to become the father-in-law of our King Stephen, the last of the Norman dynasty in England. The relations between Normandy and the south of Italy were no less close. No direct marriage indeed took place between the princely houses of Normandy and Italy; but Count Roger married a distant relation of the Conqueror. The real connexion, however, is to be found in the intercourse between the two countries. This is illustrated by the similarity of the government of Sicily with that of Norman England. We find a justiciary and a constable mentioned in Sicily as early as the middle of the twelfth century, and the Sicilian kings also had an exchequer, the idea of which was probably borrowed from Normandy or England. But through the Church lay the chief bond of union. Many a Norman and English ecclesiastic wandered south, and became bishop in Apulia or Sicily. The architecture of Normandy may have borrowed the pointed arch from the Saracen buildings of Sicily; while in the southern churches we easily detect the Norman mouldings and tracery. Norman monasteries were founded by Guiscard in Italy, as dependencies of St. Evroul. Hence a constant intercourse between Normandy and Italy, and from the chronicle of Ordericus Vitalis, the monk of Evroul we learn much of the Norman doings in Italy, and the Norman view of the Crusades.

Thus, then, the first Crusade may under one aspect be called a great Norman family alliance; and though the Lorraine interest was greatest at Jerusalem, that of the Normans of Italy affected in no slight manner the character of the expedition itself.

The members of this family coalition severally represent the various types of crusaders and the divergent motives under which they acted. Godfrey of Bouillon and Tancred of Sicily are fair representatives of the religious devotees who entered upon the Crusades as others had gone upon pilgrimages, in the simple spirit of devotion, and yearned to win back the Sepulchre from the sacrilegious hands of the Turks. Robert of Normandy best represents the wild spirit of adventure which found so congenial a field in the crusading wars. His impatience of restraint had led him to quarrel with his father. His carelessness had brought Normandy into anarchy and reduced himself to penury. And now, with the same indifference to the future, he had pledged his ducal crown of Normandy to his brother, and went on a crusade, not to win a dominion in the East, but only to satisfy his roaming love of knight-errantry, eventually to return once more to trouble Normandy with his bad government, and finally to end his foolish life in durance at Cardiff. In Bohemond we see the type of those who joined the Crusade for motives of self-aggrandisement. To Bohemond, a calm and cold politician, politics stood in the place of religion; he used the religious enthusiasm others to carry out his long-cherished schemes of conquest. The eldest son of Robert Guiscard, he had taken a prominent part in his father's wars against the Eastern Empire. On his death, Guiscard left Apulia to his second son Roger, while to Bohemond was granted the principality of Tarento and Bari, with the traditions of his father's exploits—the hope of winning an empire in Dalmatia, Epirus, and Thessaly. To Bohemond, therefore, the Crusade appeared as an opportunity of pressing his political schemes, and of gaining a principality, if not in Thessaly, at least somewhere in the East, perhaps even of winning Constantinople itself If we may believe the chronicler William of Malmesbury, he urged Urban to the Crusade for this very purpose; and his future policy shows clearly that he cared nothing for the success of the ostensible objects of the Crusade.

Such were the many-sided interests which, for a short time united, led to the first Crusade. Into the details we cannot enter. Suffice to say, that the close of the eleventh century found a Frankish kingdom founded on the shores of Palestine: Godfrey of Bouillon King of Jerusalem; Baldwin, his brother, at Edessa, in Mesopotamia; Bohemond, with a semi-independent principality, at Antioch; and Tancred, holding the city of Caipha on the seaboard.

Thus, then, with the first Crusade the Norman power reached its climax. The Norman not only ruled in England and Normandy,

Apulia and Sicily, but had spread to the far East, and was the first to plant his foot on the shores of Palestine, where no European had ruled since the days of Heraclius (A.D. 628).

Meanwhile in England Rufus had been enjoying the material prosperity so often permitted to the wicked. He had triumphed over the Scots and the Welsh. The last rebellion of his nobles had been ruthlessly crushed. The Church was completely at his feet. Anselm had been driven from England in 1097. Thomas, Archbishop of York, who enjoyed a precarious greatness in consequence of the exile of Anselm, was on his death-bed, and William had in his hands all the domains of the archbishopric of Canterbury, those of the bishoprics of Winchester and Salisbury, together with those of twelve or more of the richest abbeys of England. Freed thus from the restraint of those who would have been his censors, he openly spoke of turning all ecclesiastical property into fiefs, declared that he would become a Jew if they could beat the Christians in argument, and daily became more reckless and profane. 'Never day dawned,' says his chronicler, 'but he rose a worse man than he had lain down; never sun set but he lay down a worse man than he had risen.' Yet, in spite of his wickedness, he had energy and ability. Had these been only directed to better ends, England might have blessed instead of cursing his name. As it was, the feudal nobility were at least kept down; the incorporation of Cumberland with England, which may be dated from his reign, as well as the conquest of South Wales, were lasting additions to the strength of his country; and the Tower of London, completed by him, and the noble Hall of Westminster, built at this date, still stand as memorials of his greatness. Abroad he was equally successful. Anxious to gain the allegiance of Normandy against the return of Robert, his government there, in contrast to that of England, was discreet and moderate. Order and justice, both neglected by his careless brother, were restored, and the country flourished. The vacant abbeys and sees were all filled up. The royal domains, which had been dissipated by the extravagance of Robert, were restored, and the Norman barons who held lands in Normandy and England quietly acquiesced in an undivided allegiance. Strong in Normandy, he waged a successful war against Philip of France, and soon gained the castle of Gisors, an important outpost surrendered by Robert, Maine indeed he never gained. This, the first conquest outside the duchy made by William I., had never acquiesced in the Norman rule. Profiting by the disturbed condition of Normandy under Robert, it had once more rebelled, under Helie de la Fleche, nephew of Count Herbert, and renewed its allegiance to the Count of Anjou. Though Rufus once retook Maine, his authority was never recognised, and the county was not secured to England till the reign of Henry I.

In spite, however, of this repulse, the power of Rufus increased day by day, until, puffed up by his successes, he spoke of conquering Ireland

and claiming the throne of France, even of taking Rome itself.

From these ambitious dreams he was suddenly called away by an ignominious death. Among the acts of his father none had caused more misery or stirred more deeply the heart of the English against him than his cruel clearing of the New Forest for the deer he loved so well. Under his son, the Forest laws and courts had been used as engines of tyranny. There arbitrary custom prevailed. The courts were presided over by special officials, who were irresponsible, except to the king, and laws were drawn up rather for the protection of the beasts of chase than of the king's subjects. On one occasion Rufus had refused to accept the verdict of the ordeal by which fifty Englishmen had freed themselves from the accusation of poaching, declaring that God was no judge of offences against the forest laws. Cursed by such laws as these, the fair glades of the forest were looked upon as haunted, and fatal to the Conqueror's family. There his son Richard had died a mysterious death, and there another Richard, son of Robert, had fallen at the beginning of the year by an ill-aimed bolt. Numerous portents warned the king that his end was near. Even he himself had been terrified by an awful dream. But William heeded not: 'Do they think me an Englishman to put off a journey for an old wife's fancy?' he cried; and from a last wild debauch, he went forth into the forest to die. Whether he was slain by the accidental aim of Walter Tyrrel, or by falling on the point of an arrow as he stooped over his prey, or by the hands of some of those half-starved peasants whose homes had been destroyed to yield him sport, none can say. He died unloved and unblessed. His body, dragged into Winchester by one sorry horse, found indeed a grave amongst the old kings of England, but received no Christian burial; and when, a short time after, the tower of Winchester fell, men said it was a sign of God's wrath, because his cursed body had found a resting place within that sacred pile.

CHAPTER XVI.
HENRY I. 1100-1135.

During the reign of Rufus, Henry had lived partly in Normandy, partly in England. In Normandy he held the castle of Domfront and the Côtentin, which he had bought from the needy Robert. Enjoying here almost independent power over one-third of the duchy, he had spent his time in pleasure with his mistress, Nesta, princess of South Wales, and in literary pursuits, by which he stands in marked contrast to the rest of his family. Thus occupied, and in occasional visits to England to join in the pleasures of the chase, he had taken little part in the quarrels between his brothers, but waited with well-concealed impatience until the time should come for the fulfilment of his father's prophecy. And now the day had come. He had been hunting in the New Forest when his brother was killed. On hearing the news, he rode at once to Winchester to secure the royal treasure, and claim the crown; and so opportunely had the death of Rufus happened, that some even whispered that the murder had been done at his instigation.

Robert, having failed to gain the crown of Jerusalem, was now on his way home, bringing with him his Italian bride, Sibylla of Conversana. A few days more, and he would have been again in Normandy to demand the crown by the terms of the treaty of Caen (1091). But Robert still was absent; the title to the crown was not yet hereditary, it was held, therefore, that an interregnum ensued upon the death of the king. From the last king's death till the proclamation of the new king's peace, all law was at an end, and none could be punished for their lawless deeds. In the face of the universal hatred which Rufus had inspired, and the many smouldering elements of anarchy which existed, this was a forcible argument in Henry's favour, and his promptitude and energy did the rest.

In vain William of Breteuil pressed the claims of Robert in the interest of those Norman nobles who now as ever wished England and Normandy to be united on account of the personal advantages to be gained thereby. He was overruled. The form of election was gone through by the barons who were on the spot, and Henry hastened to London to secure that important town, and to press on his coronation.

Conscious of the weakness of his title, Henry shrewdly saw that the crown was to be won and held only by ready conciliation of all classes. Hence he forthwith granted a charter, which was the first granted by the Norman kings, and was considered so valuable that it formed the basis for the future Magna Carta of the reign of John. 'Know ye,' the charter begins, 'that by the mercy of God and the common counsel of the barons of the whole realm of England, I have been crowned king.' Having thus acknowledged the elective character of his crown, he proceeds to specify the abuses of the late reign and to forbid them for the future. The barons are conciliated by the restriction of the feudal dues and aids. The reliefs are to be moderate; the lords' rights of wardship and marriage are defined. Widows are to be allowed their right of dower. Tenants by knight service are freed from all demands except service in the field; and the barons are allowed to bequeath their personal property by will.

The lower vassals are conciliated by the promise that their over-lords shall do the same to them as the king did to the tenants-in-chief.

To the people peace and good coinage are promised. The fines are to be moderated, the arrears of debt due to the crown remitted. The laws of Edward the Confessor, by which is meant the old institutions, shall be re-established, with such amendments as had been made by his father, with the consent of his barons. But forests as they were in the Conqueror's time are retained with the consent of the barons. To the Church he promises that he will not keep the property of vacant benefices, and that he will free them from all unjust exactions. Nor was this all. Anselm was immediately recalled, the bishoprics were filled up by good appointments, and the oppressive minister Ranulf Flambard, to whom much of the misery of the past reign was attributed, was called to account and imprisoned. Finally, Henry's marriage with Matilda, daughter of Malcolm of Scotland, niece of Edgar Ætheling, and thus heiress of the Saxon line, was looked upon as a pledge that he meant to rule as an English national king.

In these conciliatory measures of Henry I. we see how fortunate it was for England that the crown was not yet hereditary, and the value of these early disputed successions. Had the sons of the Conqueror succeeded him by strict hereditary right, the crown would have been absolutely despotic. But as it was, each king was forced to lean upon the people, to impose restrictions on his own irresponsibility, and to acknowledge his people's rights and his own duties.

The Norman barons, however, resented this English policy; especially were they indignant at Henry's marriage with Matilda. They called the couple sneeringly 'Goodrich and Godiva,' and, assisted by Ranulf Flambard, who had escaped from the Tower, they invited Robert to claim his own. The invasion was skilfully managed, and many of the barons, headed by Robert of Belesme, Count of Alençon in France and Earl of Shrewsbury in England, and William of Warenne Earl of Surrey, flocked to his standard when he landed at Portsmouth.

But the English stood true to Henry. Among the barons, Robert, Count of Mellent, afterwards Earl of Leicester, his brother the Earl of Warwick, and Roger Bigod supported Henry's cause. Anselm threatened the Church's excommunication, and Robert, fearing to try the chance of a battle, consented to a peace, which he once more resigned the crown of England, and contented himself with the full possession of Normandy and 3,000 marks a year. The quarrel which afterwards ensued between the two brothers was no longer about the crown, but about the power of enforcing obedience on those Norman barons who held property in both countries. In its course it clearly illustrated the absolute necessity either that Normandy and England should be under the same ruler, or that the Norman barons should choose whether they would be English or Norman subjects, and cease to pay a divided allegiance. If every feudal rebel could fall back upon his possessions in Normandy when driven from England, and there prepare a new rebellion against the king, there could be no hope for the peace of either country.

No sooner therefore had Robert retired than Henry turned upon the barons who had defied his authority. William, Count of Mortain, who claimed the earldom of Kent as nephew and heir of Odo of Bayeux, and Ivo of Grantmesnil, who had attempted to introduce the right of private war into England, were driven from the realm. Robert of Belesme, Earl of Shrewsbury, who had long been one of the most factious of the nobles, held out in his castles of Shrewsbury, Arundel, and Bridgnorth, until Henry marched against him with the whole force of the nation, and forced him to fly and retire to Normandy!

The joy of the English at the fall of these nobles is seen in the triumph of the chronicler Orderic Vitalis: 'Rejoice, all England and King Henry, and thank the Lord God, for you became a free king on the day when you banished Robert of Belesme.'

To all these exiles Normandy, under the weak Robert, offered a tempting refuge. Joining with the disaffected nobles there, they reduced the country to a state of utter anarchy. The people filled the churches with their property to save it from the marauding barons. The power of Robert was at an end, and he himself was plundered by his rebellious vassals so that he often lacked bread to eat, and was forced to lie in bed for want of clothes to wear. The cruelties of Robert of Belesme surpass belief. He is said to have impaled men and women, and out of wantonness to have plucked out the eyes of a child as he held it at the font.

Henry accordingly interfered, and complaining that his brother had broken his treaty by sheltering the exiles from England, he invaded Normandy. He was bought off by the cession of the County of Evreux, but two years afterwards he again landed in Normandy to win the battle of Tinchebrai, where his brother and William Count of Mortain fell into his hands. The Count of Mortain was blinded, and Robert, sent a prisoner to the castle of Cardiff, spent the rest of his useless, aimless life in honourable captivity. Robert of Belesme, who in 1112 fell into Henry's hands, also remained a captive till his death.

Thus once more were England and Normandy united. Henry apparently did not assume the title of duke until his brother's death, at the age of eighty, in 1134. But from the battle of Tinchebrai he undertook the government of the duchy. His policy there forms a contrast to that pursued in England. In

England he confiscated the estates of all who rebelled. In Normandy, with a few exceptions, he contented himself with garrisoning their castles lest by more extreme measures he might throw the Norman nobles to the side of his jealous suzerain the king of France. Thus when Robert of Belesme died, he allowed his son William Talvas to succeed to the Norman estates of his father. By these wise measures he reduced the nobles to obedience and the country to peace, and, in spite of several wars with the King of France, Normandy enjoyed a security which it had never known under the restless, careless hand of Robert.

At this time Wales demanded the attention of Henry. Constant border warfare had continued there between the Welsh and the Lords on the Marches, and the Welsh had joined the rebellion of Belesme. The means adopted by Henry to increase English influence in Wales were twofold. First he attempted to subordinate the Welsh Church to Canterbury by pressing his nominees into the Sees and forcing them to receive consecration from Canterbury, a policy which was deeply resented by the Bishop of St. David's who claimed metropolitan authority. Secondly, he established in Pembrokeshire a colony of Flemings who at this time were flocking to England, driven from Flanders by one of those inundations of the sea which occurred periodically in their low-lying home. This settlement, near Tenby, did something to introduce the knowledge of the woollen trade and agriculture into Wales, and formed a nucleus of order and advance. But insurrections still continued, and Wales was never quiet until entirely subdued by Edward I.

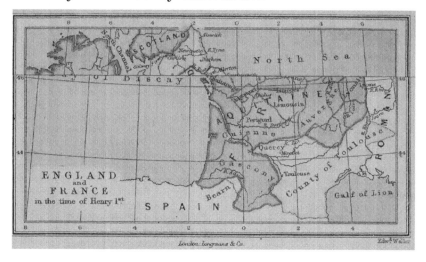

Meanwhile in England Henry had been engaged in a quarrel with Anselm. Since the reign of William I. a death struggle had been carried on between Pope and Emperor on the question of investitures. The claim to invest the bishops with the ring and crozier, the ecclesiastical symbols of office, had formed a crucial point in the system of Gregory VII. The Church was to be free from the secular power, and dependent on the Pope. But how could this be, how could simony be checked, and a recurrence of the shameful abuses of the reign of Rufus prevented, unless the Pope had the undisputed right of thus confirming or annulling elections? This was the papal view; and Anselm, coming fresh from the Council of Rome where lay investiture had been condemned, refused either to accept the symbols of his office from lay hands or to pay the homage demanded by the king. When the demand was made, Anselm referred to the canons of the Church. Henry answered, 'What have I to do with a Roman canon? No one shall remain in my land who will not do me homage.' Cherishing the customs of his father, he was determined not to abate a jot of his authority over the Church; he would exercise that authority more decently than his brother, but that was all. Anselm, true to his papal views, held to his refusal. Unsatisfactory negotiations ensued with Paschal II., who was anxious, if possible, to prevent a quarrel with a new foe until he had humbled the Emperor; and Anselm once more went into exile, to meet only with lukewarm support from the Pope. In 1105, however, Henry, anxious to gain assistance in his Norman war, and fearing the threatened excommunication, once more recalled the archbishop, and the following year saw the question settled, as it was sixteen years afterwards between Pope and Emperor at the Diet of Worms. By this compromise the Pope retained the right of investing with the ring and crozier, while the king was to confer the temporalities of the see and receive the oath of fealty from the bishop. Had the king gained the exclusive right of investiture, the independence of the Church would have been endangered; she would have become feudalised and subservient, and thus lost the secret of her moral influence. Had the king surrendered all, the Church would have formed a separate power within the realm, owing allegiance to a distant superior, and have gained a freedom dangerous to the State. As it was, Pope and King obtained all they could reasonably desire: the king was secured in his just right as feudal lord, the bishops could not deny their allegiance in temporal concerns or rebel without breaking their oath of fealty. The Pope could check the growth of simony, and enjoy the supremacy over his clergy as head of the Western Church. The Church, connected with the rest of Christendom and the ecclesiastical centre at Rome, retained her power and vitality. The quarrel had been useful in other ways. In the resistance of Anselm to Rufus and Henry we see the first constitutional opposition to the irresponsible power of the king. By it the king was taught that there was a limit to his power, an authority above him with which he must reckon, and the people learnt their right and duty of resisting arbitrary rule.

The general ecclesiastical policy of the king was marked by the same spirit of compromise.

The Pope had long claimed the right of sending legates into the country as his representatives. These legates did not interfere with the ordinary duties of the archbishop, but were invested for the time with the extraordinary powers enjoyed by the Pope alone. In virtue of this they took precedence of the archbishop, superintended the ecclesiastical synods, and administered the more important affairs of the Church. This right was not denied; but Henry, conscious that the due independence of the Church might thus be encroached upon, insisted that his consent should first be obtained before the legate could land. The synod might be called when the archbishop chose, but the king's sanction must be obtained before they could meet. The chapters were to enjoy their right of election; but the election must be in the king's court, and after his *congé d'élire.* In every point Henry maintained the principles of his father's customs, and asserted his position as ruler of the national Church; but within these limits the freedom of the Church and the papal supremacy were allowed, and in the exercise of his control Henry's conduct was dictated not by caprice, as in the case of the of William Rufus, but by the dictates of a wise and consistent policy. Anselm did not long survive his return. The rest of his life was devoted Anselm to the administration of his See, and the celibacy on enforcement of the celibacy of the clergy. In this he pursued a more rigorous course than Lanfranc. The married clergy were driven from office, and the act of marriage condemned as absolutely sinful. But the national feeling was always against the papal view; it was constantly evaded, and Anselm's attempt did not meet with complete success. He had been all along striving to establish the system of Hildebrand in England, a system which was distasteful to the English, and therefore he never entirely succeeded; but in the reign of Rufus he had boldly stood forth as the champion of a higher morality against a wicked tyrant, and his opposition to Henry was marked by the same purity and singleness of motive.

The ecclesiastical history of the reign is also marked by the foundation of two new sees, those of Ely (1109) and Carlisle (1133), and the introduction of the Cistercian order of monks into England. This order, founded by an Englishman, Stephen Harding, at Citeaux in Burgundy (1109), devoted themselves to agricultural pursuits, while the earlier orders had betaken themselves chiefly to the towns. The reign of Henry I. saw three of their monasteries established in England: those of Waverley in Surrey (1128), Rievaux in Northumberland (1131), and Fountains in Yorkshire (1132). In England the Cistercians became great sheep-farmers, and many of our most famous houses belonged to the order.

No sooner was the question of investiture settled than Henry was called abroad. The possession of Normandy brought Henry into immediate contact with France, where Lewis VI. was ruling, the first of those great princes to whom is due the ultimate overthrow of feudalism. As a boy he had been sent to the English court with sealed letters from his stepmother, in which Henry was requested to kill him. Henry had declined to do so, and thus had a claim to the gratitude of his suzerain. But personal ties gave way to motives of public policy. The power of England threatened France, and Lewis returned to the traditional policy of the French kings in supporting rebellions against the overgrown power of his vassal. The state of Normandy gave him the opportunity to interfere. The disaffected nobles disliked the firmness of Henry's rule. The doubtful claim of Henry to supremacy over the Counties of the Vexin, Evreux, and Alençon, were fruitful causes of dispute. Fulk of Anjou, ever jealous of the Norman power, again claimed the supremacy of Maine on the death of Helie dela Fleche, who had acknowledged the right of Henry. Baldwin VII. of Flanders joined the coalition, and a pretender to the duchy was found in William Clito, son of Robert of

Normandy. Success, however, smiled on Henry's arms. The Count of Anjou was bought off by the marriage of his daughter to William, Henry's only son. Robert of Belesme fell into Henry's hands, and Lewis, defeated by Theobald of Blois in the interests of Henry, submitted to the treaty of Gisors, by which he abandoned the cause of William Clito, and acknowledged Henry's lordship over Brittany, Alençon, and Maine. Henry then strengthened his position by the marriage of his illegitimate daughter to Conan of Brittany, of his legitimate daughter Matilda to the Emperor Henry V., while the acknowledgment of his son William as his heir was wrested from the barons of England and Normandy.

War, indeed, broke out again, and once more Baldwin of Flanders, Fulk of Anjou, and Lewis supported the cause of the son of Duke Robert. But Henry was again successful. Baldwin was killed, Fulk was again won over, and a skirmish at Brenneville, in which Lewis was defeated, brought the second war to a close.

At this moment the death of Henry's son William threatened to undo the painful work of years. As he was returning in triumph to England, the ship in which William sailed was wrecked off Barfleur. The prince had managed to gain a boat and pushed off from the sinking ship, but the cries of his sister recalled him to the wreck. The boat was capsized by the rush of the despairing crew, and one alone survived to bring the news to Henry. Crushed by this sudden loss, Henry is said never to have smiled again.

The death of the Prince was a severe domestic affliction; but that was not all. He was Henry's only son, and no woman had yet ruled in England; thus the hopes of seeing his family established in England received a cruel blow. The ties of interest which bound Fulk of Anjou to Henry were destroyed by the death of William, who had been married to the daughter of the Angevin count, and Fulk once more took up the cause of William Clito. His daughter Sibylla was affianced to the pretender. Lewis

VI. again threatened to join the coalition, and Henry was forced to engage in another war in Normandy. But fortune favoured him once more. Fulk shortly after resigned his estates to his eldest son, and, marrying the heiress of the kingdom of Jerusalem, accepted that precarious crown. The rebels were discomfited, and three years afterwards the death of William Clito rid Henry of the only competitor for the duchy of Normandy. Maine, which had been a source of continual trouble to William and his sons, was definitely secured, and Henry's rights as lord over Brittany were acknowledged.

The prophecy of William was now fulfilled, and Henry enjoyed a larger dominion than that enjoyed by the Conqueror himself Normandy and Maine were at last definitely united to England. These Continental dominions formed part of the English kingdom until they were finally lost in the reign of John. But this triumph, though increasing the power of the English king, was not a benefit to the English people. It once more made England part of a great Continental kingdom, to which her own interests were likely to be sacrificed. It gave the nobles increased power, the results of which were seen in the succeeding reigns. During that of Stephen, for instance, the long wars were due chiefly to the nobles who hoped thereby to increase their independence, and in the reign of Henry II. the power they had thus gained was once more used to rebel against the strong anti-feudal government of the king. Lastly, English nationality could never be established until England was split off from Normandy and the Continent, and left alone to work out her national life for herself.

Secure at last in the possession of Normandy and England, Henry now turned his attention to the question of the succession. Matilda, his wife, had died in 1118. He had afterwards married Adelais of Louvain. His new wife, however, bore him no child, and it remained to secure the succession of Matilda his daughter, who, on Matilda, the death of her husband, the Emperor Henry V., had returned a widow to her father's court. The barons were ordered to swear allegiance to her, and shortly afterwards, anxious to secure the alliance of Anjou, Henry married her to Geoffrey, the son of Fulk. By this means he hoped to win the friendship of the house of Anjou, always so hostile to the Norman power, as he had done before by the marriage of his son William. But the barons declared that their oath of allegiance had been given on the promise that Matilda should not marry a foreigner without their consent, and the hereditary jealousy of the Normans for the Angevins caused many of them to abandon Matilda for the cause of Stephen on Henry's death.

Henry was still in Normandy arranging the disputes caused by the marriage when he died, it is said, from eating too heartily of a dish of lampreys.

Amid the constant wars which had disturbed his reign, Henry had found time to improve the administration of the country; and his reign of thirty-six years forms a prelude to that of

Henry II. in this as in many other respects. In fact, the three reigns of William I., Henry I., and Henry II., the three great organizers of feudal England, stand closely together.

In Henry's quarrel with Anselm the same principles were involved as in William's dispute with the Pope, and these were again to appear in the quarrel of Becket and Henry II., though the combatants had somewhat changed their ground.

We have seen the quarrels between the king and his feudal nobles, which had begun in the reign of William, continued in that of Henry I. The reign of Stephen undid much of Henry's work which was left for Henry 11. to complete. In this struggle the kings, in spite of the arbitrary character of their rule, had been striving for the good of the country; the feudal nobles aiming to establish their independence at the cost of the nation's welfare. It was well for England that her early kings were so strong, for else she might have suffered from the evils of Continental feudalism, and her history might have been a counterpart to that of France.

In the administration of justice and in the organization of the executive power, the same connexion between the reigns is seen, the same anti-feudal tendency appears, and one reign is illustrative of the other. Henry's father had continued the Anglo-Saxon local courts of the Hundred and the Shire. During the reign of William Rufus they had been suffered to fall into disuse. The nobles probably had tried to encroach upon their jurisdiction or to get rid of them entirely, and under Ranulf Flambard they had been used for the purposes of fiscal extortion, and thus became objects of suspicion to the people themselves. These courts Henry now revived, and promised that for the future, when he had need of money, he would not demand it at the ordinary sessions, but summon these courts especially for the purpose. The local courts thus revived, it was necessary to draw them closer to the central court of justice—the Curia Regis introduced by William his father. The means resorted to were these. The duties of the Curia Regis and its financial committee were systematised, the offices of the justiciary and those of his staff of justices organized. By his circuits to the local courts their dependence was secured. Already the justices, his subordinates, began to take his place, and making their eyres (circuits) chiefly to superintend the collection of the royal dues, and therefore in their office as Barons of the Exchequer, led the way for the definite establishment of Justices in Eyre by Henry II. In some cases the justices were made sheriffs of several counties, and thus presiding in the regular sessions of the Shire courts, connected them closely with the central court of the king. To carry on this work new officers were required, and Henry, neglecting the old nobility who had, by their continual rebellions, forfeited all title to his confidence, turned to the lower ranks of the noble order. Thence he created a class of ministerial families who furnished the sheriffs of the counties, the justices of the Curia

Regis, and the barons of the exchequer, and greatly facilitated Henry's policy. They were, indeed, unpopular, but for that very reason they served Henry's purpose all the better. They were bound by interest to the crown; they were not too powerful to be brought to justice, and their acts were closely criticised by nobles and by people. The most important of these new ministers was Roger, Bishop of Salisbury. Henry had first met him when a poor priest in Normandy. Attracted, as the story runs, by the wit which the poor priest had shown in discerning his impatience to hasten to the hunt, and satisfying it by shortening the service, Henry made him his steward and chaplain. Here his great powers of administration were displayed, and finally he rose to be Bishop of Salisbury and justiciary. The choice was wisely made. To Roger is chiefly due the fiscal organization of the office and of the Curia Regis, the control of which remained in his family for nearly a century.

While thus advancing the administration of justice and introducing order and routine, Henry was not regardless of other interests. His charters to the towns mark a step in the growth of municipal life, and a wise recognition of their claims. His police, too, was good. The system of frankpledge was maintained and developed. By this everyone had to find a surety; if he was a vassal, his lord was answerable; if a freeman, the association of freemen to whom he belonged. The false coiners were heavily punished, and a new coinage issued.

In every way the reign of Henry I. was a gain to England. It marks a distinct advance in the growth of national life, and in the progress of arbitrary but good administrative government; and it is to Henry's credit that he has earned the title of the Lion of Righteousness.

But withal Henry was an irresponsible despot, and loved to be so. With all his father's military and administrative sagacity, he was more cruel and perhaps even more tyrannical. He refused to give up the forests; those who dared gainsay him or rebel against him were punished with merciless rigour, and Henry would listen to no will but his own.

His great judicial reforms are probably to be attributed to no higher motive than the love of order and the desire to increase his revenue by the fines of the courts. Hence his heavy taxation, a continual source of lament in the chronicles of the reign. 'The manifold taxes never ceased. He who had any property was bereaved of it by heavy taxes, and he who had none starved with hunger.' His wars in Normandy, his wars against his nobles, all are to be referred to his overmastering selfishness. But, fortunately for England, that selfishness was clear-sighted and far-sighted, and his own private aims tallied with the interests of the nation. The nobles were his enemies; he destroyed them, and in doing so destroyed the enemies of the nation. Anarchy was hateful to him; he substituted the reign of routine, and thus prepared the way for law, which might in time itself set a limit to royal irresponsibility.

Thus, while the people could not love him, they respected and they feared him, and this accounts for the varying characters left of him by the chroniclers. 'Men thought differently about him,' says Henry of Huntingdon, 'and after he was dead spoke their minds:—some spoke of splendour, wisdom, prudence, wealth, and victories—some of cruelty, avarice, and lust.' The lower classes were very miserable throughout his reign; the constant wars rendered taxation necessary; a series of bad harvests and stormy seasons made the burden heavier.

Henry, in spite of the support given him by the English, was at heart a foreigner. No Englishman found a place amongst his ministers. No Englishman found preferment in the Church. The two nations were gradually uniting, so that in the reign of Henry H. we are told it was difficult to distinguish between them; but yet the English found no recognition of their claims at the hand of their Norman king.

And yet, while the English complained, they instinctively supported the king, acknowledged that he sought for peace, and saw that their only hope lay in strengthening the royal power and thereby crushing the feudal nobility.

'Inflexible in the rigour of justice, he kept his native people in quiet and his barons according to their deserts,' says William of Malmesbury; while Henry of Huntingdon tells us 'that in the evil times that followed, the very acts of tyranny or of royal wilfulness seemed in comparison with the worse state of things present most excellent.'

Henry was the last of those great Norman kings who, with all their vices, their cruelty, and lust, displayed great talents of organization and adaptation, guided England with a wise if a strong hand through the days of her youth, and by their instinctive though selfish love of order paved the way for the ultimate rise of a more stable yet a freer government.

That, however, was yet in the womb of the future, and the Norman period closes in the anarchy of Stephen's reign.

Of that reign we do not intend to treat. It forms rather the prelude to the reign of Henry II. The Norman era really ends with Henry I., for Stephen was only a Norman by the spindle side, as was Henry II. the Angevin, and throughout the reign all constitutional history is at a standstill.

It is a period unexampled in English history, a period during which England suffered all the ills of Continental feudalism.

Amidst the anarchy of the civil war, the nobles covered the country with their castles, set authority at defiance, fostered the continuance of discord for their own ends, and strove to establish their selfish independence.

In the misery which ensued, the lower classes, both Norman and English, were learning their identity of interest against such men as these, with whom they felt that no truce could be kept. Painfully but surely they were drawn together into a close national unity, and to an intense yearning for peace which led them one and all to welcome the strong rule of Henry II., and any government which might crush out for ever this hateful Continental feudalism. Thus the reign of Stephen, though it closes the Norman period in sorrow and shame, was yet a valuable discipline for the country, and formed a secure basis for the reforms of Henry II., who took up the work where Henry I. had left it, and completed it.

We have now traced the course of that great Scandinavian exodus, which, beginning in the ninth century, spread over the whole of Europe. Having briefly sketched the fortunes of the less important branches, we have devoted especial attention to the settlements in France, which assumed the specific name of Norman. After following their fortunes in France we have accompanied them in their various settlements in Spain, Italy, and England. Finally concentrating our attention on the latter country, where their genius receives its most forcible development, we have traced the connexion between it and Normandy, and in greater detail drawn out their influence on our country and the principles of our government. With the reign of Henry I. the Norman kings reached their highest pitch of power. After him their kingdom passed away—first to the house of Blois, then to that of Anjou. With both these houses they had long been connected, with both an hereditary and deadly hostility had existed from the earliest times. But though the Norman power thus slipped away from the direct descendants of Rollo, the Norman influence was not destroyed in England. They never were driven out. They coalesced with the English, and lost their individuality in the common nationality; but they long enjoyed the chief positions in the state, and the Norman administrative and executive machinery still lies embedded in our constitution side by side with the local institutions of the Anglo-Saxons.

It will be well at the close of our survey to cast our eyes abroad, and take a last glance at the condition of the other Scandinavian or Norman powers. The continents of Denmark, Sweden, and Norway had long settled down into organized communities, and for half a century had not troubled Europe. Norway still enjoyed her nominal sway over the Orkneys, the Shetlands, and the districts of Sutherland and Caithness in Scotland, these not being ceded to the Lowlands till the middle of the fifteenth century.

In Iceland the free republic was on the point of being dismembered by the rise of an aristocracy, and one century later was once more to be occupied by Norway, To the west of Scotland lay the sovereignty of the Isles, consisting of the Hebrides and other islands along the coast, as well as certain settlements in Anglesea, Man, and Ireland. This kingdom, under the Lords of the Isles, owned allegiance to Norway, but was virtually independent. Of these Anglesea and Ireland fell to England in the reign of Henry IL, Man long enjoyed semi-independence under its own' lords, while the

Hebrides were ceded to Scotland in the latter half of the thirteenth century.

In Italy the Norman kingdom of Apulia and Sicily still belonged to the descendants of Robert Guiscard, and maintained constant intercourse with England. Under this line of kings it continued until the end of the twelfth century, when their dominion passed away, with the hand of Constance the Norman heiress, to the Emperor Henry VI.

In Palestine the Norman nobles still held some fiefs; and the Frankish name was to continue there, but with fast declining power, until the end of the thirteenth century (1291). In Russia the descendants of Ruric still sat on the throne of Kiev, until they should be subdued by the Tartar invasion of the same century (1240).

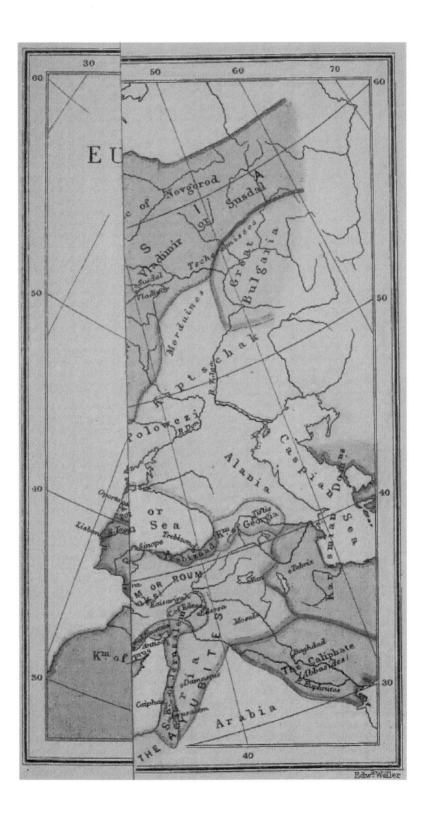

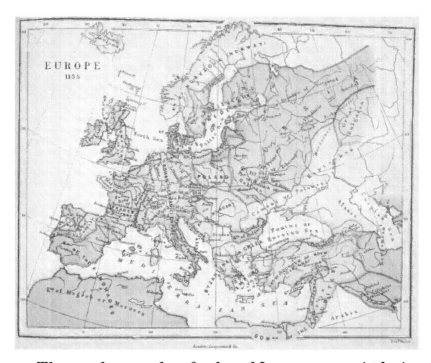

Thus the end of the Norman period in England nearly synchronises with that of their rule elsewhere. They had been the leaders during a most important epoch of European history. They had seen the foundation of most of the future great European powers. For two centuries at least they had been the most influential people in Europe. They had formed the nucleus of cohesion amidst the fluctuating state of European nationalities. Wherever they went they had shown themselves great warriors, founders, organizers, and administrators. With extraordinary powers of adapting themselves to outward and altered circumstances, they had, while adopting the systems of their conquered subjects, developed them, added to them, and perfected them. To them France owes the establishment of her national kings, nay almost her very existence as the kingdom of France; southern Italy a dynasty under which she enjoyed a prosperity denied her since; Russia a long line of powerful and clever princes; Iceland a free republic; England a stern and harsh schooling indeed, but a useful one—stern law, the suppression of anarchy, the establishment of order and excellent administration—all essential preliminaries of true progress.

And now their work is over. The Norman period is fast waning. New ideas, new forms of government, new systems are to arise, and the great impulse which originally had come from the Scandinavian continents is exhausted.

CHAPTER XVII.
NORMAN ADMINISTRATION.

The great constitutional work of the Anglo-Norman period was, as we have seen, the organization of administrative routine.

The Norman king was virtually a despotic sovereign. William gained England at a time when the theoretical powers of the Anglo-Saxon king were at their highest, and to these he added the prerogatives of the feudal sovereign without the practical limits which abroad were found in the independence of the feudal vassals. The nobles enjoyed none of the semi-royal rights of jurisdiction or taxation in their domains, and when William I. exacted the oath of homage from every subject at the Council of Sarum, he destroyed even the authority which the feudal vassals abroad enjoyed over their sub-vassals.

The Witenagemot, which under the Anglo-Saxons had served as a constitutional check on the powers of the king, was turned into a feudal court, the creature and the servant of the sovereign. The king became the lord of the land and the source of all justice, and there was no authority in theory or in practice which could gainsay his will, One limit alone remained: the crown still in theory remained elective, and the right of deposition was preserved. Hence the kings, as in the case of Rufus, Henry I., and Stephen, were forced to secure their title by concessions, which, unfortunately, there was no constitutional means of enforcing.

The king thus powerful in theory and in practice, the chief interest in Norman times necessarily centres round his person, and all that England then gained must be attributed to the royal authority and to the officials who surrounded him. The most important of these originally were the High Steward, the Chamberlain, the Constable, officers exclusively of the royal household, which, though not without analogies in Anglo-Saxon times, had been copied by the Norman dukes from the old officials of the Karolings. Of these officers, the High Steward or Seneschal acted as supreme official in the royal court; the Chamberlain was the financial officer of the royal household; the Constable was the Quartermaster General of the royal army; he mustered the forces and ordered their disposition on service, he paid the mercenaries, and had jurisdiction over offences against the laws of war and other disputes m the army. The Constable subsequently shared his powers with the Marshal, an officer of later creation, who, besides the share he had in the duties of the Constable, took especial cognisance of disputes in the court itself.

The Steward, the Constable, and the Marshal each had their separate courts independent of the common law, and in later times these were the object of much complaint, as interfering with the right of a subject to be tried by his peers.

By the side of these officers of the household there rapidly arose a ministerial class who soon supplanted them. The household offices became hereditary in certain families definitely in the reign of Henry II., and fell back into an honourable position, but one of secondary constitutional importance.

The ministerial officers are chiefly these: the Justiciary, the Treasurer, the Chancellor. Of these the Justiciary was, in the Norman times, by far the most important. The origin of the office is obscure. It was unknown abroad before the Norman Conquest, and was therefore of purely Anglo-Norman creation. The first Justiciary was William Fitz-Osbern, the steward or seneschal of William, and this has been taken as an indication that the origin is to be sought in the seneschalship, the duties of which were transferred to this new office. However this may be, Ranulf Flambard, the oppressive minister of William Rufus, must be considered the first consolidator of the office, and Roger of Salisbury, the famous, minister of Henry I., the final organizer of its duties. His powers, growing side by side with the advancing centralisation of government, when they reached their climax in the reign of Henry I., were these:—He was, *ex officio*, regent of the kingdom in the king's absence. He was the president of the Curia Regis, and of its financial committee or session, the Exchequer, and he united in his own person all the rights and duties of supreme financial, judicial, and executive officer.

He was surrounded by a number of officers, who, when sitting in the Curia Regis were called Justices, but in the Exchequer, Barons of the Exchequer.

Representing the king, the Justiciary went his circuits, by which he kept the local courts in due subordination, watched over the financial privileges of the king, and held periodical gaol deliveries.

Already in the time of Henry I., as we have seen, his own officers or justices were beginning to take his place owing to press of business and increasing centralisation, to become under

Henry II. the itinerant Justices, with regular and fixed circuits.

The Justiciary from the time of Ranulf Flambard was universally an ecclesiastic, probably to prevent the great powers of the office from becoming the prerogative of any one family, or in any sense hereditary, and because churchmen alone could be trusted to administer these distinctly antifeudal duties faithfully.

Next to the Justiciary came the Treasurer. To him was entrusted the keeping of the royal treasure at Winchester. He was an important officer in the Exchequer, and received the accounts of the sheriff in that court.

The Chancellor. This officer, who in after times became the most important of all, and the second subject of the realm next to the Archbishop, stood only third in Norman times.

The office appears in England as early as the reign of Edward the Confessor, and was probably derived from the archicancellarius of the Karolings. The derivation of the name; the 'cancelli,' or screen behind which the secretarial work of the household was carried on, tells us of his duties.

He was the Secretary of State and chief of the clerks of the king's court. Always an ecclesiastic, he held the position of chief chaplain to the king. He kept the king's conscience, as the phrase went, and administered the revenues of vacant benefices until they were filled up.

All these officials were members of the Curia Regis. This term seems to be applied indiscriminately to the committee of the Commune Concilium, and to the supreme judicial court of the realm, and it is by no means improbable that they were originally one Regis, and the same. 'The committee of the national council administering justice in virtue of the king's assumed presence there, or the king's judicial court usurping the legislative functions of the national council.'

It is, however, with the Curia Regis as a judicial court that we are now concerned. Again many opinions have been held as to the origin of this court. Some claim for it a purely Saxon origin, and as a judicial look upon it as representing the committee of the old Witenagemot. By others it is declared to be of purely Norman growth. The truth seems to lie between. No doubt the Dukes of Normandy had their Curia Ducis, or feudal court, in common with other feudatories. This they brought with them to England, and uniting it with the committee of the Witenagemot turned it into the Curia Regis. For the rest, its powers were of gradual growth, and, as they appear under Henry I., were different at once from its Anglo-Saxon and Norman prototypes a court of Anglo-Norman creation and organization with 'a double origin.

The Curia Regis then, as a judicial court, was the court of the king sitting to administer justice with his counsellors. These were theoretically all the members of the national council—practically, the great officers of state, and a few expressly summoned justices; and in the absence of the king, it was presided over by the justiciary. Its original jurisdiction extended to disputes between the tenants in chief, and in other cases where leave had been obtained. But its more important duties belonged to it as a court of appeal from the inferior courts. In this way the local courts were united to the central courts, and this connexion was much increased when the justices of the supreme court became itinerant justices, or were made sheriffs, as was the policy of Henry I.

When sitting for financial purposes it was called the Exchequer, and since in Norman times the financial necessities of the king were the primary motives in developing the judicial system, this its financial side was the most important. At the two full sessions held at Easter and Michaelmas, the sheriffs appeared and paid the farm of the shire, each county's share of the Danegeld, the proceeds of the pleas of the crown, and the feudal dues; these, with the sale of offices and exactions under the Forest laws, forming the chief incidents of Norman taxation. The *Farm of the Shire* was the sum for which the shire was let to the sheriff, who reimbursed himself from the royal dues, the fines in the court, the profits from the royal demesnes, or from other sources. The *Danegeld* was a tax levied since Anglo-Saxon times for the defence of the realm, but much increased by William I. and Henry I. The *Pleas of the Crown* were special offences, the fines of which went directly to the crown; especially the *murdrum*, or sum of money payable by each hundred in cases where a murder had been committed within their limits. By William I. this was exacted in cases where the murdered man could not be proved to be an Englishman, and the verdict which settled this was called the Presentment of Englishry.

Of these accounts the Treasurer and the Chancellor each kept an account, termed the Pipe Roll of the Treasurer, and the Roll of the Chancellor.

Cases of dispute were settled by the Barons of the Exchequer, who went their circuits for this purpose, and these were probably the origin of the later judicial circuits of the Justices in Eyre.

Under the central court, with its two sides, judicial and financial, worked the local courts of the shire, the hundred, and the manor. These were continued from Anglo-Saxon times, and the procedure remained the same, with, the addition of the trial by combat in cases where Normans were concerned, and the inquests by sworn jurors for the purpose of gaining information, such as that required for the compilation of the Domesday Survey, for the assessment of taxation, and for the settlement of disputes concerning land.

In the Shire court, presided over by the sheriff, the king's nominee, greater causes, civil and criminal, were tried.

The Hundred court, presided over by the bailiff, settled small disputes of debt; and when presided over by the sheriff, was termed the Sheriff's leet in criminal matters, the Sheriff's tourn, for holding views of frank-pledge in connexion with the system of police.

The bond between these courts and the central court was very slight at first, and it was the work of the Norman period to draw it tighter. William I. had for this purpose resorted to the custom of holding three annual sessions of the Curia Regis in the three great towns of the south, Westminster, Winchester, and Gloucester. Henry I. sent his Barons of the Exchequer to sit in the county court for the assessment of revenue. The Justices in his reign also began to go their circuits, and were often themselves made sheriffs, by which the subordination of these local courts was effectually secured.

Besides these popular courts, there existed also the Manorial courts, the Forest courts, and the Courts of the enfranchised boroughs.

The manor was nothing more than the ancient township which had now fallen to a feudal lord. They had, as before shown, virtually existed in Anglo-Saxon times, in the case of those thanes who had gained independent rights of jurisdiction conveyed by the grants of sac and soc. In Norman times they were so much increased that nearly the whole of England was divided into manors, either of the king or belonging to some lord, with the exception of a few enfranchised boroughs.

These manors would be thus divided: part the lord would keep for his own use under the name of the demesne; the rest would be granted out to freehold tenants on varying terms of tenure, or would form the waste over which the lord retained the right of sporting, while the tenants of the manor might there feed their cattle or cut their turf and peat. Of the demesne again part was retained in the actual occupation of the lord: his park and farm, which was termed the demesne proper. On the rest his villeins would be settled. Bound to the soil, they might not' leave it, and in return for their small holdings they had to till the demesne proper. If the land were sold they passed with it.

In these manors the old town-reeve had given up his place to the steward of the lord, but in other respects the procedure was the same as in the popular courts. The rights of jurisdiction varied according to the terms of grant. All had their Court baron, representing the Gemot of the Anglo-Saxon township, in which by-laws were passed and local business transacted; and all their Customary court for the business of the villeinage. In these cases the lords were not exempt from the jurisdiction of the Hundred court. Others would have by grant Courts leet for criminal purposes, and others a right to hold views of frank-pledge, as they were called, when the manor would be free from the Courts leet and tourn of the sheriff respectively.

In some great baronial jurisdictions, which included almost the whole shire, the lords enjoyed entire independence of the sheriff and the Shire court, and the suitors to their courts exemption from all attendance at the popular courts. The number of these greater jurisdictions, which were hereditary, always had a tendency to increase, and were dangerous not only as decreasing the profits of the popular courts and the crown, but as serving as a basis for baronial tyranny in such times as those of Stephen. There was no means of checking them except by increasing the central power, and it was not till the reign of Henry II. that they were compelled to admit the Justices of Eyre to exercise jurisdiction in them.

There was no privilege to which the Norman kings clung so closely, or which caused so much misery and discontent, as their exclusive right of enjoying the sport in the royal forests. William had desolated the New Forest with cold-blooded indifference, and the curse had been visited on his family. Rufus had much increased the forests. Even Henry refused to part with any when he had to appeal to the people in his charter, and added more to their number. At a somewhat later date it was computed that there were 67 forests, besides 30 chases and 781 parks. Over these the jurisdiction was vested in the Forest courts. Here a distinct system of law prevailed. They were ruled by royal officials, independent of the ordinary judges of the popular courts and Curia Regis, not bound by the common law, and irresponsible except to the king. Their laws and customs were their own, and variable, until Henry II. issued the first Forest code, even then marked by such severity that it is said the punishment for breach of forest law was heavier than for heresy. Nothing proves more strongly the arbitrary rule of the Norman kings, or their selfishness, than the stubbornness with which they clung to their forests and Forest courts.

In Anglo-Saxon times some of the more fortunate boroughs had gained an exemption from the Hundred court, and enjoyed their own rights of jurisdiction in their ward and borough motes, with an organization similar to that of the popular courts. They still, however, remained subject to the Shire court, and the sheriff collected from them the royal dues. By the Norman Conquest they fell into the demesne of some great lord or of the king, and the status of citizens exactly corresponded with that of the inhabitants of the rural districts, those who held property being termed 'burgage' tenants, corresponding to the 'socage' tenants, and the lower class of citizens to the 'villeins' of the rural manor. For any further advance they now had to look to the grant of the lord or king in whose demesne they lay. Those who were not rich enough to buy these privileges, or were on the demesnes of some lord who had not the power of granting these immunities, remained much in the condition in which the Norman Conquest found them, and survive to the present day in our market towns, with an humble machinery of police and magistracy in connexion with their markets. The more privileged gained their charters from king or lord. Having won independent jurisdiction, the next step was to procure an independent administration. This, as was so often the case in Norman times, first took the form of a fiscal question. Hitherto the sheriff had himself compounded for the dues of the boroughs in the farm of his county, and levied the dues upon the town himself, and to his own profit. Probably in many cases more was exacted than was legal; but the towns had no remedy. It was natural, therefore, that they should wish to compound directly with the king or lord, and thus be freed from the common valuation of the shire. This was done by obtaining charters, by which the burghers themselves rented the borough dues, paying to the king or lord the rent of the borough (firma burgi), and collecting it themselves from the citizens. Thus they were freed from the exactions of the sheriff, and changed their varying dues into a fixed and certain rent. The grant of the ferm implied an emancipation from 'villein' services; and, since the ferm was generally granted to the ward-mote of the town, all members of that court, holders of land or houses within the borough, henceforth held their land on free 'burgage' tenure. This, with a few other privileges, was all that was gained in Norman times.

Side by side with the growth of the boroughs, the system of guilds had arisen. For the origin of these we must look to Anglo-Saxon times. The distinguishing feature of early Teutonic society lay in its strong spirit of local organization, in itself probably a remains of the old family tie. As this family tie became weakened, they seem to have sought for some other personal bond, founded on the analogy of the family, which might take its place. Hence the rise of guilds which appear universally in Western Europe, taking various forms, of which the following are the most important.

Religious or social guilds.—These were probably the earliest, and resorted to for some religious purpose, such as prayers for quick and dead, burial of their dead, representation of miracle plays, alms, and good works. Others again formed friendly societies for mutual help and protection. 'If one misdo,' runs one of their by-laws, 'let all bear it: let all share the same lot.' Others, under the name of Frith guilds, formed assurance companies against loss or theft, to give compensation when any member had suffered, and to avenge all insults as common ones. It is to these Frith guilds that we probably owe the idea which afterwards led to the system of frank-pledge. At times all these objects would be united in one guild. The existence of such associations as these, and their rules of membership, speak highly for the peace and order loving character of the people; and as they survived the Norman Conquest, they affected our after history. No rebel or man of bad fame might be enrolled a member, and such offences worked instant forfeiture; while a rule from a guild of later date speaks highly for their moral and industrial influence: 'If any man fall poor from using to lie long in bed, and at rising off his bed will not work but go to the tavern, wine, ale, wrestling, and in this manner falleth poor, that man shall never have help or good of the companie neither in life or death, but shall be put out of the companie.'

As trade increased, the same spirit of association led to the rise of *merchant* and *craft guilds*. Of these the *merchant guilds* probably existed in some few cases before the Conquest, but rapidly increased during the Norman period. They were associations of merchants uniting for purposes of mutual assistance in trade. They gained by charters the monopoly of trade, and then gradually obtained the virtual government of the towns by the following means. The guild, including as it did all the important men of the town, would necessarily be members of the borough courts; thus the members of the guild and the governing body of the town would be composed of the same persons, and guild law would tend to become town law. But further, in some cases the merchant guilds seem themselves to have purchased the 'firma burgi,' and in virtue of this would have the right of assessing the contributions upon the citizens. Thus membership in a merchant guild would be indispensable for the full status of a burgher, who thereby gained a stronger spirit of co-operative union. Still the governing body of the town and the guild were not as yet identical. Their organization was separate, and the influence of the guild was indirect rather than actual or avowed.

Beneath these merchant guilds, the lower craft guilds, or associations of craftsmen, had begun to arise; but for their future development, and the consequent struggle between them and the merchant guilds for the municipal government, we have to wait for a later date.

The towns then in Norman times had gained an independent jurisdiction, some independence of administration in fiscal matters, and various privileges. But they were still subject to the Shire court; they were in no sense a corporate unity, as they subsequently became, and their organization was still that of the rural hundreds and townships.

The condition of London was, indeed, somewhat more advanced. By the charter of Henry I. it received the 'ferm' of the whole county of Middlesex, with the right of appointing the sheriff. The citizens were freed from all jurisdiction of any other Shire court, and from the obligation of trial by combat, together with other privileges and immunities. They had their folk-moot, answering to the Shire court elsewhere: their ward-mote, corresponding to the rural Hundred courts; and their 'hustings court,' or weekly meeting of the citizens in common. Still even London, though far in advance of any other towns, had no municipality as yet. It was, in fact, a civic shire, as the other towns were civic hundreds; and under their folk-moot, or Shire court, the several townships, parishes, and manors of which it was composed, retained their separate jurisdiction and organization.

The military system of the Norman kings was threefold.

(1) The Anglo-Saxon organization of the militia was retained. By this, every man was bound to serve the king on foot in times of danger. They were marshalled under the sheriff of each shire, and each man received the sum of 10*s.* from his county to meet the expenses of his service.

(2) To this the Normans added the feudal levy, by which every tenant by knight service had to furnish one fully armed horseman for forty days in the year, when summoned by the king, either on home or foreign service.

The baron led his own knights, and the host was marshalled by the Constable and Marshal; those knights who held immediately of the crown appearing with the militia under the sheriff.

(3) These levies were further supplemented in time of war by foreign mercenaries of footmen and archers. Thus William I. hired mercenaries to resist the invasion of Canute of Denmark in 1085; and Stephen's employment of Flemish and Breton mercenaries, at the outbreak of the civil war, alienated many of his partisans.

We have spoken of the probable relation which the Curia Regis held to the Commune Concilium, or national council.

This national council is to be considered as a continuation of the Anglo-Saxon Witenagemot, under the character of a feudal court.

Theoretically, all freeholders holding in chief of the crown were members, and on a few great occasions, as at the Council of Salisbury, 1085, such general musters would be made. But in those days, attendance at the royal councils was looked upon as a burden rather than a privilege; and its ordinary members would accordingly be confined to the archbishops, the bishops, abbots, earls, barons, and knights; and of these probably only a limited number of the more important would of the ordinarily appear.

The abbots and friars sat in virtue of their holding a barony of the king, the archbishops and bishops as being besides the chief advisers of the crown.

The earls, originally the successors of the Anglo-Saxon earls, whose numbers, at first small, were increased in the reigns of Henry I. and Stephen, gained their dignity by special investiture of the sword of their county by the king. The proceeds of jurisdiction they shared with the sheriff, receiving a third of the fines arising in the Shire court.

The barons were the successors of the king's thanes of Anglo-Saxon times. They held in chief of the king, and enjoyed a dignity sometimes personal, sometimes territorial. The class was composed of many grades, varying according to their personal qualifications, official duties, and extent of property.

The knights, representing the old thanes, were really the lesser barons, in fact the whole class of tenants by knight service.

The powers of the council thus formed, theoretically extended to legislation and taxation. The king acknowledged 'its counsel and consent' in the former, and in the latter probably laid before it any rather than plan for increasing the existing taxes. But, practically, the king was absolute, and its counsel and consent a mere form.

The council, however, still enjoyed certain powers. These courts were held annually on the festivals of Easter, Pentecost, and Christmas, at the towns of Winchester, Gloucester, and Westminster, respectively, when the king wore his crown before his subjects.

It formed a court of judicature for trying peers, as in the case of Waltheof, in the reign of William I., and of Robert of Belesme in that of Henry I.

Here also the following business was transacted. The bishops were nominated, until Henry I. granted the right of free election to the chapters; here the earldoms and other dignities would be conferred; questions of policy discussed and ecclesiastical canons ratified, though the archbishop often held an ecclesiastical council at the same time, where the canons themselves would be prepared.

Even in these matters the council probably did little more than give its formal assent, and the only point in which its authority was practically exercised was in the election of the king. On those occasions the royal authority was in abeyance; the nation resumed its rights, only to lose them again as soon as they had elected their future master.

Thus the Norman king enjoyed an authority, confined indeed within certain theoretical limits, but practically irresponsible, and the government might not be inaptly described as a despotism Norman tempered by the elective principle.

Of the administration of Normandy during this, as in the earlier period, we have but scanty evidence. All the authorities, of which the Grand Coutumier of Normandy is the most important, are of later compilation; and of original charters, rolls, or other documents, there is a curious dearth.

We may be sure, however, that there was a close connexion between England and Normandy at this date; though, probably owing to the disturbed condition of the duchy, England was considerably in advance.

We have noticed before the analogies between the Curia Regis and Exchequer of

England and the Curia Ducis and Exchequer of Normandy.

No doubt England here borrowed largely, especially in the forms of procedure, from her foreign sister. But so had she done from Anglo-Saxon institutions, and the debt of Normandy to England was probably as great.

Of the municipal life in Normandy again we know but little. We hear of sworn communes, and Le Mans had wrested privileges from William as early as 1073. But in common with the rest of France, the object of municipal freedom in Normandy was more distinctly political than in England, and a comparison of the few charters which remain leads us to the conclusion that in this as in other matters the advantage lay with England.

In conclusion, the question how far England and Normandy borrowed each from the other will best be answered if we remember that it was a period of transition and of growth in both countries, and that the administrative systems of each country grew together.

GENEALOGICAL TABLES

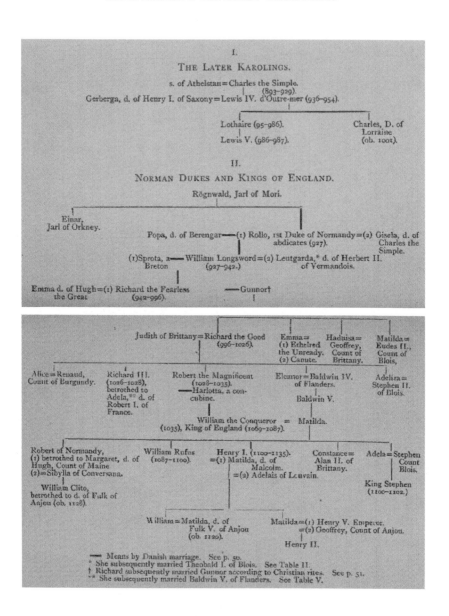

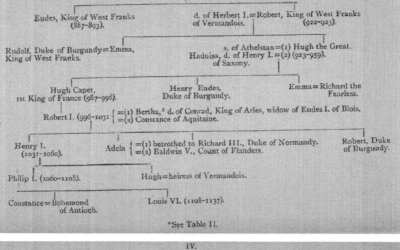

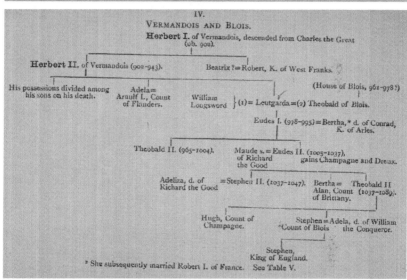

V.

COUNTS OF FLANDERS.

Baldwin I., Bras de Fer = Judith, d. of Charles the Bald.
(858-879).

Baldwin II. = Elfrith, d. of Alfred.
(879-918).

Arnulf I. = Adela, d. of Herbert II. of Vermandois.
(918-964).

Baldwin died before his father, 962.

Arnulf II. (973-988).

Baldwin IV. the Bearded = Eleanor, d. of Richard the Good.
(988-1036).

| Baldwin V. De Lisle = Adela,¹ . of Robert | | Judith = Tostig, br. of |
| (1036-1067.) f France. | | Harold. |

| Heiress | Baldwin VI. (1067-1070). | Robert Le Frison. | Matilda = William |
| of Hainault. | = I. of Hainault. | (1072-1092). | the Conqueror. |

(2) Baldwin II. of Hainault	(1) Arnulf III. of Flanders	Robert II.	Adela = Canute of
(1070-1126).	(1070-1072), deposed.	(1093-1111).	Denmark.
		Baldwin VII.	
		(1111-1119).	

¹ She had been betrothed to Richard III., Duke of Normandy. See Table IV.

VI

ANJOU.

Ingelger 870 ?).

Fulk the Red (888-931).

Fulk II., The Good (938-958).

Geoffrey I. (958-987).
Grisegonelle.

Fulk Nerra (987-1040)

| Geoffrey Martel | d. = Geoffrey, Count of |
| (1040-1060). | Château Laudon. |

| Geoffrey II. (1060-1066). | Fulk IV. Rechin (1066-1109). |

d. of Helie de la Flêche (1) = Fulk V.,	(2) = Melisenda, heiress	d. = Alan Fergus,
King of Jerusalem	of Jerusalem.	Count of
(1109-1129 ; ob. 1141).		Brittany.

Matilda = William,	Sibylla,	Geoffrey IV. = Matilda, d. of Henry I.,
son of Henry I.	betrothed to	(1129-1151). widow of Emperor
	William Clito.	Henry V.

Henry II., King of England
and Count of Anjou.

Made in the USA
Lexington, KY
02 September 2017